Grimsby at War

1. Fish and chips for tea? A boat pulls away from HMT *Northern Sky* to collect fresh fish from the Grimsby trawler *Andros* (GY5)

By Clive Ha

D1354274

First published 1989 by
Archive Publications Ltd
10 Seymour Court
Manor Park
Runcorn
Cheshire WA7 1SY

in association with the

Grimsby Evening Telegraph
80 Cleethorpe Road
Grimsby
South Humberside DN31 3EH

© 1989 Text Clive Hardy
© 1989 Photographs Grimsby Evening Telegraph

ISBN: 0-948946-50-4

2. Macauley Street School, 1941.

Introduction

The purpose of this book is to present a photographic record of life in wartime Grimsby and Cleethorpes, and to show something of the way in which the Second World War directly affected the lives of every man, woman and child. It is not meant to be a definitive work in any way but an attempt to recapture the atmosphere of fifty years ago, when this country fought for its very survival against Nazi aggression, and, for a whole year, alone.

As well as looking at everyday life in and around Grimsby, which was forced to adapt to the stringent demands of war with the rationing of food, fuel and clothing, the book has also tried to capture something of the experiences of local men and women enlisted in the services, who may have spent the whole of the war away from their families. There are sections devoted to Grimsby's trawler fleet, HMS *Grimsby*, the Lincolnshire Regiment, the Grimsby ATS, RAF Waltham and Victory & Beyond.

The photographs and information have been drawn from a wide range of sources, but a special mention must be made for the staff of the *Grimsby Evening Telegraph* who researched and compiled the *Bygones Series*. I wish to thank George Black and Pat Otter in particular for their help and enthusiasm, and wish to acknowledge the work of David Tilley, Vincent McDonagh, Claire Beal, Geoff Ford, Malcolm Smith, Jim Wright, Tim Rayment, Betty Korsak, Frank McNought, Nicola Joules, Ray Simmons and Mike Howden.

Clive Hardy
July 1989

3. Workmen taking up tramlines in Cleethorpe Road for recycling for use in the war effort.

TAKE THE PLUNGE

WHY KEEP YOUR UNWANTED ARTICLES?

"SMALLS"

RADIO - PAGE 4

Grimsby Evening Telegraph

LARGEST CERTIFIED NET SALES IN LINCOLNSHIRE

FINAL

No. 15,812 FRIDAY, SEPTEMBER 1, 1939 ONE PENNY

DON'T OVERLO

Look over them n

HITLER STARTS WAR ON POLAN

Warsaw Bombed: Many Civilians Killed

POLES INVOKE TREATY WITH BRITAIN

GENERAL MOBILISATION AND MARTIAL LAW IN FRANCE

A.R.P. IN FULL FORCE : SIRENS FOR AIR RAID WARNINGS ONLY

HITLER has set his war machine in motion against Poland. Warsaw and other towns have been raided from the air, and Danzig has been taken over to the Reich.

Following an alleged "rejection" by Poland of terms for negotiation, Germany has acted with lightning speed. From Paris and Warsaw come reports of the Nazi Army and Air Force attack.

Official quarters in London say that "Great Britain and France are inflexibly determined to fulfil to the utmost their obligation to the Polish Government."

REUTER'S DIPLOMATIC CORRESPONDENT LEARNS THAT THE POLISH AMBASSADOR SAW LORD HALIFAX THIS MORNING. HE INFORMED HIM OF THE GERMAN ATTACK UPON POLAND, WHICH, HE SAID, CONSTITUTED A CASE OF DIRECT AGGRESSION AS PROVIDED BY THE ANGLO-POLISH TREATY, WHICH HE INVOKED.

HE KING HAS SIGNED AN ORDER IN COUNCIL FOR COMPLETE MOBILISATION OF THE ARMY, NAVY AND AIR FORCE.

N FRANCE GENERAL MOBILISATION HAS BEEN DECREED AND MARTIAL LAW PROCLAIMED.

A Polish Embassy official said to-day that the towns bombed by German planes were taken completely unaware. "Nobody supposed there was war. Without any declaration of war, they have bombed our Polish cities."

he German offensives are developing in three directions:—

(1) FROM EAST PRUSSIA.

(2) TOWARDS SILESIA AND

(3) NORTHWARDS FROM SLOVAKIA.

arsaw and six other Polish towns were bombed by German warplanes this morning. Reuter learns from Polish sources.

e raid on Warsaw occurred at nine o'clock. Many of the civilian population are reported to have been killed and injured.

ITLER, ADDRESSING THE REICHSTAG TO-DAY, SAID: "WE MUST ABOVE ALL THANK ITALY, WHO HAS SUPPORTED US . . . BUT THEY WILL UNDERSTAND THAT I WILL NOT APPEAL TO FOREIGN HELP IN THIS FATEFUL HOUR.

We will carry out this our task ourselves." In his speech the Fuehrer announced Danzig's union with he Reich.

ONFIRMING A GENERAL OFFENSIVE LONG THE ENTIRE POLISH FRONT, OFFICIAL AT THE POLISH EMASSY IN LONDON TOLD A PRESS SSOCIATION REPORTER: "I THINK HE EUROPEAN WAR WILL START O-DAY."

e spoke these words on the News Agency tapes came flashes of ported German attacks on the Corridor and Polish towns. Upper esia is also being attacked.

Both the British and French Cabinets were meeting this morning, and both Houses of Parliament were summoned for 6 o'clock to-night. At 1 p.m. the King was holding a Privy Council.

while the greatest exodus in history goes on as 3,000,000 children, thers, blind and maimed persons and hospital patients are being cuated in Britain.

uesday it is hoped that all these people will be safe in the event war.

dramatic proclamation to the German army, broadcast by the cial German wireless to-day, Herr Hitler announced: "From now I have no other choice than to meet force with force. The German y will fight the battle for the honour and vital rights of reborn rmany with hard determination."

A few minutes later came news that the Free City of

GREAT BRITAIN IS READY

SUPPORT FOR POLAND

IT is pointed out in official circles in London that if the proclamation to the German people by Herr Hitler, which has already been announced, should mean as it would seem to mean, that Germany has declared war on Poland, it can be stated on the highest authority that Great Britain and France are inflexibly determined to fulfil to the utmost their obligations to the Polish Government.

"The German account of the course of the negotiations is, of course, wholly misleading. On August 29 the German Chancellor informed H.M. Ambassador that he expected a Polish plenipotentiary to appear in Berlin by the following day, with full powers to negotiate a settlement. He added that in the meantime he hoped to elaborate proposals.

CZECH PRESIDENT

"In other words, the Polish Government was expected to submit to the procedure imposed on the President of Czechoslovakia and to despatch an Emissary to Berlin who was to accept terms, the character of which was wholly unknown to the Polish Government.

"The Polish Government has not unnaturally been unwilling to place themselves in this humiliating position.

"It is not customary, even in the case of peace terms imposed on a defeated Power, to demand that negotiators should not be allowed to refer for instructions to their Government.

"It is impossible to comment at such short notice on the misleading statements of the German Government, but the general attitude of H.M. Government may be briefly defined as follows:

"If the German Government had been sincerely desirous of settling the dispute by negotiation, they would not have adopted this procedure which has the character of an ultimatum.

"They would, on the contrary, have opened negotiations with the Polish Government in accordance with the normal procedure of civilised governments, in order to fix the place and time for the opening of negotiations.

FULLY JUSTIFIED

"The Polish Government, in the opinion of H.M. Government, were fully justified in declining to submit to the treatment which the German Government endeavoured to impose on them.

"As regards the terms now published, which have never been hitherto communicated to the Polish Government, H.M. Government can only say that these terms should, of course, have been submitted to the Polish Government with time to consider whether or not they infringed Poland's vital interests which Germany in a written communication to the British Government had declared her intention of respecting."

POLISH PRESIDENT AND "PROPER REPLY"

WARSAW, FRIDAY

President Ignacy Moscicki of Poland broadcast the follow proclamation to the Polish nation to-day:—

"Early this morning Germany launched an attack on Polish State.

"In this historic moment I appeal to all our citizens w the deep conviction that the whole nation will, in defence of freedom, independence and honour, rally round the supre commander of the armed forces, and give a proper reply to German aggressor, as it has so often done in the past.

"The whole nation, conscious that the blessing of Almighty rests on its fight for a sacred and just cause, and uni in the army, will take up the struggle until victory is complet

ADVICE TO THE PUBLIC ON SHELTER IN AIR RAIDS

THE following hints and information are issued for the benefit of the public in regard to the best forms of protection against bombs in an air raid.

First of all, it should be borne in mind that the direct effects of a high explosive bomb—that is, the effects which cause major destruction—extend over a very limited range, not further in most cases than a 30ft. circle round the bomb.

It may be assumed that if as many as 50 bombs of the largest size fall in a square mile, any individual within that square mile would have something like a hundred-to-one chance of escaping what may be called the "direct hit effects."

It is the secondary effects, that is, splinters—including splinters of shells from anti-aircraft guns—blast, and the fall of debris, which are liable to cause by far the greatest number of casualties in an air raid, and the individual can do a great deal to protect himself against such effects.

ERECT SHELTERS

Anyone who has an Anderson shelter properly earthed over is virtually secure from anything except a direct hit, or its equivalent. Therefore, anyone who has a shelter not yet erected should see to its erection at once.

Those who have no garden shelters can obtain a considerable degree of protection by digging a trench in the garden with 18 inches of overhead earth cover.

It should be remembered that the ordinary dwelling house offers a good deal of tion. The side walls, or one or t overhead, will stop most splinters. ber that well-constructed buildings easily brought down unless a big bo very close indeed.

People should not be upset by pic what happened to the poorly built h Spain.

SHELTER IN THE HOUS

The best place inside the house basement, or if there is no basem ground floor. Choose a passage or with a small window for the place of especially if it looks out on a narrow

Small or narrow rooms are bett large ones. If it is necessary to c room, choose a position where splint ing through the window will not hit a

On no account look out of the w during an air raid. The stick stout paper or adhesive tape cris on the glass or windows will great duce the danger from flying splint broken glass. Windows are bes open if there has been no gas war

So much for those who are at hom the warning sounds.

(SHELTER OUT OF DOOR

Anyone who is out of doors should any signs leading to public basem trenches. Otherwise seek shelter in a stantial building. Remember, agai any such building offers good pr against anything but a virtual hit. A passage between buildings, an area stout archway will give protection. in any event remain standing or r about in the street.

NEWS OF THE FIGHTING

From All Sources

NEWS of Germany's attacks on Polish towns was contained in the following messages.

WARSAW. — Polish towns of Cracow and Katowice have been bombed from the air.

Germans also attacking Upper Silesia.

PARIS.—Warsaw was bombed 9 a.m., Reuter learns.

WARSAW.—Official Warsaw radio announced Germans launched full scale attack against towns in Polish Corridor.

HELSINKI.—According to reports reaching here some fifty German planes took part in the bombing of Katowice, Silesia, to-day.

PARIS.—Polish towns bombed are Vilna, Grodno, Brzesc, Lodz, Katowice and Cracow. Before the air attack German troops had crossed the Polish frontier, apparently between 6 and 7 a.m., at four points, including [illegible] frontier.

WARSAW.—German planes attached Poland in two waves this morning. In the first Kutsk, Gdynia, Thorn, Bialystock, Grodno, Dibivo, and Bydgoszcz were bombed, and in the second Warsaw, Cracow, Katowice, and Czenstowice.

ENGLISH SHEEPDOGS

The team of fifteen sheepdogs to represent England at the International Trials at Edinburgh was selected to-day when the English National Trials were con-

U.S. FORCES TOLD

WASHINGTON, Friday.

President Roosevelt has ordered that all warships and army commands be notified immediately by radio that hostilities have broken out between Germany and Poland.

The following announcement was issued from the White House this morning:

"The President received word by telephone at 2.52 a.m. (7.52 a.m. B.S.T.) from Mr. Biddle, the American Ambassador in Warsaw, and Mr. Bullitt, the Ambassador in Paris, that Germany has invaded Poland and that four Polish towns are being bombed.

"The President directed that all naval ships and army commands be notified by radio at once.

"There will probably be a further announcement by the State Department in a few hours."

TENNIS TRIUMPHS FOR GRIMSBY SISTERS

Ann Tackley, of Grimsby, won the final of the women's singles, and her sister Susan won the final of the girls' singles at the Lincolnshire Junior Lawn Tennis Championships, played on the Eastgate, Lincoln, yesterday.

The results were:—

Boys' singles final: A. Boys beat Francis 6—3, 6—4.

Boys' doubles final: P. W. Colley and A. Boys beat D. Sneeting and W. E. G. Ham-

JAPAN AND TIENTSIN CONCESSION

TOKIO, Thursday.

The new Japanese Prime Minister, General Nobuyuki Abe, stated to-day that the isolation of the British concession in Tientsin was only a military necessity.

It would be lifted, he said, in the event of Britain abandoning her pro-Chiang Kai-Shek attitude.

Although the Japanese and British conversations had reached a deadlock, Japan was

IT LOOKS GOOD
IT TASTES GOOD
HEWITT'S
HB
PALE ALE
THE BEER THAT IS BEST.
HEWITT'S

5-10. The evacuation of Grimsby schoolchildren started on the morning of Friday 1 September 1939. The children assembled at their schools, the first to leave being Hilda Street, Weelsby Street and Holme Hill. The number of children evacuated was, however, far below the number expected. This was probably due in part to the evacuation not getting the final go-ahead until the afternoon of the day before, when shops were already closed and a number of parents were unable to obtain the necessary clothing and other articles for their children. Every child carried their gas mask, some food and a few personal belongings. Linen labels with their names and addresses written on them were provided by the Education Authority.

Eight single-decker buses were provided by Grimsby Corporation, but six proved ample to accommodate the children who had turned up. Teachers accompanied them. The children were marshalled in their respective groups in the playgrounds, each group being headed by a banner and bearing the number of the group and the letters *GY*.

Supplies of corned beef, chocolate, biscuits, and tinned milk had been provided by the Corporation as rations for the children

for two days.

The *Evening Telegraph* on 1 September 1939 gave the intended destination of all evacuees. Harold Street School was to go to Horncastle Urban District; Holme Hill, Hilda Street and Weelsby Street schools to Alford Urban District; Armstrong Street, South Parade and Macauley Street schools to Skegness; Little Coates School to Sutton-on-Sea and Mabelthorpe; Victoria Street, Strand Street and St Mary's to Spilsby Rural District; and St John's to Woodhall Spa.

Mothers with children under five and the physically disabled were evacuated on 2 September.

Arrangements were made at Cleethorpes for the evacuation of schoolchildren to commence on Monday 4 September, head teachers being in attendance at their schools on the Sunday so that parents might be given all the assistance they needed.

The Cleethorpes evacuation area comprised the North and Sidney Wards, and that part of the Central Ward between Grimsby Road and the sea from Neville Street up to St Heliers Road, and also the area bounded by Grimsby Road, Bramall Street, Brereton Avenue and Ward Street.

11. It's race day for Hull evacuees at Barrow-on-Humber.

NATIONAL EMERGENCY

IMPORTANT   *IMPORTANT*

BE PREPARED

EVERY PERSON—YOUNG OR OLD—
SHOULD WEAR OUR

Identity Discs

[Fu]ll Name and Address—Plainly and Permanently Engraved
[on] Aluminium—Non-Rusting—Can Be Worn Next the Body

[En]sure You and Your Family Carry On Their Person Correct
Identity Details—*ESPECIALLY THE CHILDREN*

[ID]ENTITY DISCS FOR CHILDREN—WHERE DESIRED
[TH]E EVACUATION GROUP NUMBER WILL BE SHOWN

[Ma]nufactured to be worn suspended round the neck—easily concealed

PRICE **1/-** EACH DISC

ONLY OBTAINABLE FROM

["Ide]ntity Disc," LEEDS PLACE, TOLLINGTON PARK, LONDON, N.4.

[TO] ORDER:—Forward P.O. value 1/- for EACH Disc, made
[o]ut to "Identity Disc" and crossed /& Co./, also enclose
a stamped (1½d.) addressed envelope and full details.

[IM]MEDIATE DELIVERY.   LAST A LIFETIME.

"ONLY 30/- A WEEK TO FEED FIVE"

This real-life story is based on the actual experiences of an Oxted family whose name and address can be seen on personal application.

Many other families are finding that

[G]OLD MUST BE [S]OLD TO THE [T]REASURY

[I]f you have any gold coins you must take it to the [bank] and sell it to the Treasury. Luxury imports, in[cludi]ng motor-cars, clothing and perfumery, are [bann]ed.

[Th]ese regulations were issued last night.

[R]esidents in Britain must offer foreign securities and [coi]n, as well as gold coin, to their bankers.

[Fore]ign exchange to be offered for sale includes currencies [held] by the Treasury from time to time. Those already named [are]:—

[U.S.] dollars, Guilders, Canadian dollars, [Argen]tine pesos, Belgas, Swedish crowns, [Swiss] francs, Norwegian crowns and [French] francs.

[Pers]ons may apply through their bankers for [permis]sion to retain gold and foreign exchange [neede]d to meet contracts, made before the [coming] into force of these regulations, which [allow] for payments in gold or foreign ex[change], for meeting the reasonable require[ments] of trade or business, or for reasonable [livin]g or other personal expenses.

[Pric]es to be paid for gold and foreign ex[change] offered for sale are to be determined [by the] Treasury, and may be ascertained by in[quiry a]t any bank.

[The] public should continue to transact busi[ness in] foreign exchange and gold through the [medium] of their bankers.

[Appl]ications for exchange must be made in [the ap]propriate form, and satisfactory evidence [with reg]ard to the transaction proposed must be [provid]ed in all cases.

[Expo]rt of banknotes, gold, securities or [foreign] currency is prohibited except with per[missio]n.

[Tra]ders Must Insure

[An] order issued by the Board of Trade bans [all im]ports, except under licence, of luxuries [the kin]ds of which there are sufficient home [suppli]es.

[It] will conserve exchange for the addi[tional] purchases of other products required in [wartim]e.

[The] main categories of goods covered by the [ban] are pottery and glass, cutlery, clocks [and wa]tches, textile goods and apparel (includ[ing foo]twear), certain chemicals and paints, [some] office machinery (including typewriters), [motor-]cars, musical instruments, perfumery [and to]ilet requisites, toys and games and [some] foodstuffs.

[Trad]ers in Britain who sell goods liable to [war or] enemy risks must insure them under the [War] Risks Insurance Act.

[This] is part of a scheme which the Board of [Trade] has put into operation.

[Liabi]lity of the Board as insurers will be de[termin]ed by a policy of insurance issued in a [form] prescribed in the schedule of the War [Risks (]Commodity Insurance) (No. 1) Order. [Insura]nce is compulsory except where the [value] of a person's insurable goods does not ex[ceed £]1,000.

ADVERTISER'S ANNOUNCEMENT

Armour your larder with *Armour's* VERIBEST [C]ORNED BEEF GRADE "A"

HITLER BLAMES BRITAIN

HITLER, in messages to his Army of the West and to the German people yesterday, blamed Britain for the war.

He claimed that the Poles had "attacked" Germany, and that he was fighting to "establish peace." He added that he was on the way to the Eastern Front.

To his troops on the Western Front he said (according to the German News Agency, quoted by Reuter):—

"The British Government, driven on by those warmongers whom we knew in the last war, has resolved to let fall its mask and to proclaim war on a threadbare pretext.

"For months it (the British Government) has supported the Polish attacks against the lives and security of fellow-Germans and the rape of the Free City of Danzig," continued Hitler.

"In a Few Months"

"Now that Poland, with the consciousness of this protection, has undertaken acts of aggression against Reich territory, I have determined to blow up this ring which has been laid round Germany.

"Sections of the German Army in the East have now, for two days, in response to Polish attacks, been fighting for the establishment of a peace which shall assure life and freedom to the German people.

"If you do your duty, the battle in the East will have reached its successful conclusion in a few months, and then the power of the whole Nazi State stands behind you.

"As an old soldier of the world war, and as your supreme commander, I am going, with confidence in you, to the Army on the East."

"Unity or—" Threat

To the German people Hitler said the English "encirclement" policy was resumed when the "peaceful" revision of the Versailles Treaty seemed to be succeeding.

To this he added: "The same lying inciters appeared as in 1914."

Claiming that "as long as the German people was united it has never been conquered," Hitler uttered this threat:—

BILLETS BY ORDER, IF—

A FEW householders who have so far been unwilling to receive evacuees are asked not to force the Government to exercise compulsion.

Making this appeal yesterday, Sir Warren Fisher, the North-West Regional Commissioner, pointed out:

"It is not possible at present to say how long the billets will last.

"But all must be prepared for danger and hardship, and will be lucky if it takes no worse a form than receiving strangers into one's house.

"No war can be won under modern conditions unless the essential work of the towns can be continued in spite of air raids. This will be easier if the townspeople in dangerous areas can be relieved of anxiety for their young children.

"It is also of vital importance to preserve the lives of children, who will be the citizens of the next generation, so that householders in safer districts must take them in.

"Parliament has given powers to billet them compulsorily in the reception areas, and the Government is determined to use those powers if necessary."

BANKS ARE SHUT TO-DAY

TO-DAY has been declared a limited Bank Holiday, affecting only banks. The arrangement applies to the Post Office Savings Bank and other savings banks.

This day will be used by the banks to complete their measures for adapting themselves to the emergency, and to-morrow morning the banks will be open for business.

The Treasury, in conjunction with the Bank of England, have taken all the steps needed to ensure that the banks (including the Post Office Savings Bank and other savings banks) will be amply supplied with currency.

Postal orders will be legal tender for the present, and Scottish and Northern Ireland banknotes will be legal tender in Scotland and Northern Ireland respectively.

AIR MAIL CURTAILED

Empire air mail services are from to-day restricted to two services weekly in each direction between the United Kingdom and Sydney and one weekly in each direction between the United Kingdom and Durban and between the United Kingdom and Kisumu.

Corresponding modifications will be made in the overseas connecting services operated by Imperial Airways.

Present arrangements under which first-class mail to certain countries is forwarded by Empire Air Mail services without surcharge will be suspended, and a surcharge will be imposed on all mail from the United Kingdom carried by air on the Empire routes.

Immediately after Mr. Chamberlain's dramatic broadcast to the nation, the Government yesterday announced a number of precautionary measures to prevent people crowding together and so increasing the casualty risks from air raids.

Instructions were given for the closing of all places of entertainment until further notice. In the light of experience it may be possible to open cinemas and theatres in some areas later. Included in the closure orders are indoor and outdoor sports gatherings where large numbers of people might be expected to congregate.

The following advice is given:—

Keep off the streets as much as possible; to expose yourself unnecessarily adds to your danger.

Carry your gas mask with you always.

Make sure every member of your household have on them their names and addresses clearly written. Do this on an envelope or luggage label and not on an odd piece of paper which may be lost.

Sew a label on children's clothing so that they cannot pull it off.

People are requested not to crowd together unnecessarily in any circumstances.

Churches and other places of public worship will not be closed.

All day schools in evacuation and neutral areas in England, Wales and Scotland are to be closed for lessons for at least a week from yesterday.

In the reception areas schools will be opened as soon as evacuation is complete.

PETROL IS RATIONED

PETROL rationing will be introduced, as from September [4].

This was announced last night by the Secretary for Min[es]. Information as to how the public can secure their ration boo[k] will be announced to-day.

There are very substantial stocks of petrol in the countr[y], but in the national interests the best use must be made of the[se] supplies.

Petrol distributors have arranged to pool their resources and, after the individual bran[ds] still in stock at garages and service statio[ns] have been sold by them at prices now ruli[ng] one grade only of motor spirit will be suppli[ed] to the public.

This spirit will be called "Pool" mo[tor] spirit, and will be on sale, ex-pump, in Eng[land] and Wales at 1s. 6d. a gallon.

Appeal to Owners

No change will be made in the price for t[he] next fourteen days at least. From to-day [no] further supplies of individual brands will [be] made at garages and service stations.

For at least the same period of fourt[een] days there will be no change in yesterda[y's] bulk prices to those commercial conce[rns] who receive their supplies direct.

Owners and drivers of commercial vehicl[es] are particularly asked to note that it wil[l no] longer be possibly to allow commercial vehi[cles] to call at petrol companies' depots for suppli[es].

The Government appeal to all owners [of] motor vehicles to use them only for essen[tial] purposes.

U.S. REFUGEES LEAVE LONDON

BETWEEN two and three thousand Am[eri]can refugees left London last night. Many of them were destitute.

An American Embassy official said it mi[ght] take ten days before sufficient ships [to] evacuate these people will have been put in[.]

Mr. Joseph Kennedy, American Ambassa[dor,] has requested all American and other neut[ral] steamship lines to provide all available shi[ps,] including freighters and tankers, for evac[ua]tion.

WARNINGS TO SHIPPING

Cinemas, Theatres Close to Cut Risks

The Home Front

On 28 December, the Press carried news that the rationing of meat would be introduced on 15 January 1940. W S Morrison, Minister of Food, announced that the intended ration was to be six ounces per head per day, though it was expected that this would be for prime cuts only and that cheaper cuts of beef, mutton or pork would still be available for purchase up to the value of six ounces of prime cut. The rationing would not apply to tinned meats, fowl, rabbit or 'offal'.

The rationing of basic foodstuffs was introduced in January 1940. The weekly allowance per person included two ounces of tea (non for the under fives) and two ounces of fats. Extra cheese was allowed to those workers who had no canteen facilities, and a special ration was available to vegetarians who undertook to surrender their meat coupons. Bacon and ham were rationed at 1s 11d per pound for middle, 2s 1d per pound for ham/gammon and at 1s 6d per pound for shoulder. Other cuts were priced at 1s 4d per pound for first quality top side (second quality and imported cuts were 2d per pound cheaper), 1s 6d per pound for first quality mutton and 2s 2d per pound for prime rump steak. Again, second quality and imported cuts were a few pence per pound cheaper.

In February 1942, Sir Stafford Cripps told the House of Commons that "personal extravagance must be eliminated altogether". This meant no petrol for pleasure motoring, a cut in the clothing ration and sporting events being curtailed. Cigarettes were not officially rationed but tobacconists would often sell only to regular customers (2s 4d for twenty). Silk stockings became a thing of the past and women resorted to painting their legs with gravy browning. In 1938 over 33 million pairs of stockings were imported, but by 1944 the total had dropped to just 718,000 pairs.

At the beginning of 1945 the weekly basic ration was 4 ounces of bacon, two ounces of tea, eight ounces of sugar, meat to the value of 1s 2d, eight ounces of fats, three ounces of cheese and two pints of milk. In March the milk ration was increased by an extra half pint per person per week, but by May shortages led to reductions in bacon and lard rations. The clothing ration in 1945 was 48 coupons. A man's suit made of utility cloth took 24 coupons, and soldiers being discharged early on medical grounds could make a small fortune by selling their demob outfits. The outfit included a suit that would have cost around £12 in Civvy Street, a shirt worth 25s, two collars, a tie, two pairs of socks, a pair of shoes, a raincoat and a felt hat. The army valued the whole outfit at £11. On the black market the price could be upped because the buyer stood to save 56 coupons.

GET ME OUT OF HERE — THIS IS NO PLACE FOR ME!

SQUASH HIM IN YOUR STAMP BOOK

Ha-ha! Caught at last! Nice work! The treacherous Squander Bug firmly trapped in a book of Savings Stamps. There's an end to frivolous spending. . . . Every Savings Stamp you buy helps the boys who are fighting—and is another smack at the Squander Bug!

Savings Stamps, 6d., 2/6 and 5/-, can be exchanged for National Savings Certificates, or Defence Bonds, or used for making deposits in the Post Office or Trustee Savings Banks.

ISSUED BY THE NATIONAL SAVINGS COMMITTEE

THE PATRIOTIC PRESENT

Your **SAVINGS** are **SAFEGUARDED**

with the greatest **SECURITY** possible at the local

TRUSTEE SAVINGS BANK
(Under Government control).

Place your spare money in the **BANK**!

The Savings Bank Service at all times—even in an "Emergency"—is unequalled.

Pass Books Free.
From 2½% Interest Allowed.

GRIMSBY SAVINGS BANK

(A "Trustee Savings Bank"—Certified under the Act of 1863)

OFFICES AT—
91 Cleethorpe Road.
46 Victoria Street.
44a St. Peter's Ave.,
Cleethorpes.

ATTENDANCE DAILY—
10 to 4 (Sats. 10 to 1) and on Monday and Friday Evenings from 6 to 8.

18. Meals on wheels. A WVS mobile canteen at Nunsthorpe.

1 EGG FOR YOU EACH WEEK

AN egg a week may be the "ration" when control comes into force next month. And there is no guarantee of that.

The Ministry of Food stated yesterday that until they have obtained experience of the number of home-produced eggs secured under the new control scheme, and have observed the distributive machinery in operation, it is not possible to state the number of eggs that will be available for each consumer.

They hope that everyone will be able to obtain during July at least four eggs, but no guarantee can be given.

The first allocation of eggs is being made at the beginning of the first week in July, and should be available in the shops

PART 1 IN THE POTATO PLAN

Parsley Potato Cakes

Potatoes for Breakfast

three days a week

Potatoes taste grand for breakfast. Try them! Here's a good suggestion: Parsley Potato Cakes. Are you watching out for other recipes in this series?

PARSLEY POTATO CAKES

Boil an extra pound of potatoes the day before you want to make the cakes. Mash these while hot, with a little milk, and seasoning of salt and pepper to taste.

Next day, add a tablespoon of chopped parsley and shape the mixture into little cakes. Cover with browned breadcrumbs, and pan-fry in a little hot fat, or bake in the oven. The mixture should not be made wet.

The 4 other parts of the Plan:

2 Make your main dish a potato dish one day a week.

3 Refuse second helpings of other food. Have more potatoes instead.

4 Serve potatoes in other ways than "plain boiled."

5 Use potatoes in place of flour (part potatoes, part flour).

Bread costs ships . . .
Eat home-grown potatoes instead

ISSUED BY THE MINISTRY OF FOOD, LONDON, W.1

Your kitchen rang must burn less this winter !

Get to know it better. Persuade it to do more — for less! Every scuttle saved means more for the factories, to swell the output of weapons — to finish the job.

ECONOMISE IN EVERY WAY YOU CAN

Here are some examples:

Have a fire in one room only—breakfast in the kitchen	Wrap up hot water pipes and tanks to retain heat
Never use your oven for a single dish	Waste occurs when dampers are open unnecessarily
Use less hot water for baths and washing up	Sift and use all cinders, and use coal dust for banking

Call at your Coal Office or Gas or Electricity Showroom for advice and leaflets on how to economise.

Where to go for Entertainment—
VARIETY, CINEMAS, DANCES, ETC.

PIER PAVILION
CLEETHORPES

NCOLNSHIRE SUMMER AMATEUR DANCING COMPETITION

(ficially recognised by the Official Board of Ballroom Dancing)

PRELIMINARY HEATS

in connection with the above competition will be held in the

PIER PAVILION EACH MONDAY Evening

commencing

ONDAY NEXT - SEPTEMBER 4

y Forms and Full Particulars obtainable at the PIER PAVILION.

Winners to receive SILVER CHALLENGE CUP

to be held for one year.

SEVERAL OTHER CUPS AND PRIZES

REGAL FREEMAN ST., GRIMSBY.

Week commencing
AUGUST 28th.
Continuous Daily from 2.0 p.m.

HUMPHREY BOGART — KAY FRANCIS in

KING OF THE UNDERWORLD."

Amazing drama. (Approx. 3.45—6.30—9.25) A

Also

y Singleton, Arthur Lake in " Blondie Meets the Boss " (u)
Another Hilarious Blondie Comedy. (Approx. 2.10—5.5—7.45)

ast Complete Performance commences at approximately 7.40 p.m.

RGE GIBSON at the COMPTON WONDER ORGAN.

RITZ CLEETHORPES—PHONE 61713

Open 1.45. Com. 2.0. Continuous.
Last performance at approx. 7.40.
ALL THIS WEEK

CONRAD VEIDT in
HE SPY IN BLACK " U

VALERIE HOBSON — SEBASTIAN SHAW
from the beginning : Note Times : 3.30, 6.20, 9.15

" SHARP-
SHOOTERS " u
With BRIAN DONLEVY
LYNN BARI.
A thrill with Newsreel
Cameramen: 2.0, 4.50, 7.40

NORMAN AT THE ORGAN :: 3.20 : 6.10 : 9.5

TRAND
AN A.B.C. THEATRE.

MATINEE DAILY at 2.0 p.m.
EVENINGS CONTINUOUS from 6.0 p.m.
TO-DAY

HEART OF THE NORTH" (U)

Thrilling Tale of the " Mounties." In Technicolour.

— with —

DICK FORAN :: GLORIA DICKSON.
2.50 — 6.50 — 9.5.

OLI THEATRE
GRIMSBY. Tel. 2135. An F.J.B. Theatre
Resident Manager : Teddy Glanvill

ALL THIS WEEK. 6.40—TWICE NIGHTLY—8.50

. Roberton presents his
Topical Revue

EVERYBODY'S DOING IT

NGUS WATSON : JACK LEWIS and His Rolling Stones.

O'Toole : Rex Arthur : Nancy Collins : DOLLY LEWIS : EDITH
LLINGTON : Elsie Day : Bert Cecil : Tommy Wood : 8 Jay Dee Girls 8
Something New, Novel and Original — 20 SINGING SCHOLARS 20

ight:—Theatre Royal, Lincoln: Neville Delmar's RADIO LUXEMBOURG
:—Savoy, Scunthorpe: KITTY MASTERS and JEAN DE CASALIS.

ROYAL ★
CLEETHORPES. Tel. No. 61223.
TWO SEPARATE HOUSES.

— TO-DAY —

PAT O'BRIEN and JOAN BLONDELL in " OFF THE RECORD "
With BOBBY JORDAN.

Also:—" NAVY SECRETS," with FAY WRAY and GRANT WITHERS.

PRESENTATION OF GIFTS TO BEAUTY QUEEN PRIZE-WINNERS TO-NIGHT (Second House)

By MR. TAYLOR-BROWN (Managing Editor of the " Evening
Telegraph ") and THE MAYOR and MAYORESS (Ald. and
Mrs. Rhodes).

— BOOK YOUR SEATS —

EMPIRE ★
CLEETHORPES. Matinees Daily at 2.15.
Continuous from 6.0.

— TO-DAY —

MAX MILLER in " EVERYTHING HAPPENS TO ME "
With CHILI BOUCHIER. "Cheekie Chappie" Fast-Moving Musical Comedy.

ALSO: TORCHY GETS HER MAN, With Glenda Farrell & Barton Maclane.

SAVOY
GRIMSBY

WEEK OF AUGUST 28th.
CONTINUOUS from 2 - p.m.
Doors Open 1.45.

THE FAMOUS RADIO SLEUTH !

INSPECTOR HORNLEIGH A
GORDON HARKER ● ALASTAIR SIM
3.30 — 6.25 — 9.20

JANE WITHERS in
" MISS FIX-IT " u
2.0 — 4.50 — 7.50

CAFE OPEN DAILY 11 a.m. to 10.15 p.m.
LIGHT REFRESHMENTS
TEAS, GRILLS, ETC.

PALACE •EVENING CONTINUOUS from 6.15. :: BARGAIN MATINEE each day 2.15.
(Saturdays continuous from 2.15). : To-day and To-morrow.

CONRAD VEIDT in " THE SPY IN BLACK " (U)

With SEBASTIAN SHAW and VALERIE HOBSON.
Screened to-day at 3.0, 6.55, 9.5.
(To-morrow, Saturday, at 2.45, 4.50, 7.0, 9.10).

TOWER

TO-DAY. The Vivid Drama of a Fighting Family Doctor.
ANNE SHIRLEY, EDWARD ELLIS in

"A MAN TO REMEMBER" (A)

Showing at 2.0, 4.20, 6.45, 9.10.
Also — A True Life Drama : " HIT AND RUN."

PLAZA

— TO-DAY :: 2 TOPPING FILMS 2
PRESTON FOSTER, KAY LINAKER, FRANK JENKS & Star Cast in

THE LAST WARNING

— FIRST TIME AT THIS CINEMA —

ALSO:- Robertson Hare, Alfred Drayton, George Sandes, Berton Churchill
in— SO THIS IS LONDON

Next Week:—Monday: NURSE FROM BROOKLYN. Also: Night Club Hostess
Thursday: DEVIL'S PARTY. Also: Held For Ransom.

REX
CINEMA. Corporation Road, Grimsby. Phone 4039. Car Park.
Con. Every Evening 5.45. Bargain Mats. Mon. & Thurs. at 2.15.

FRIDAY & SATURDAY : Follow the Stars at the REX—Definitely Superlative Comfort

PETER LORRE in MR MOTO'S LAST WARNING

ALSO: John Barrymore and George Murphy in "HOLD THAT GIRL."
Next Mon., Tues. and Wed.: THANKS FOR EVERYTHING, with Jack Oakie.
Thursday, Friday and Saturday: SABU in THE DRUM.

QUEEN'S
TO-DAY :: CONTINUOUS 5.45
MATINEES DAILY : 2 p.m.

CHARLES BICKFORD, BARTON MacLANE,
PRESTON FOSTER, NAN GREY in— " THE STORM "

ALSO:—CHARLES RUGGLES in— "HIS EXCITING NIGHT "
With Ona Munson, Maxie Rosenbloom and Stepin Fetchit.

Monday Next — JACK HOLT in " THE DEFENCE RESTS."

"DANZIG RET IRNS

Entertainment & Sport

It would be wrong to think that life came to a halt. True, BBC television closed for the duration of the war, but there were only two thousand or so television sets in the country and the vast majority of these were in the London area. However, nine out of ten homes had a radio set and the reorganised BBC Home Service was to produce some memorable programmes including *ITMA; Band Waggon; Garrison Theatre; Hi Gang!; Workers' Playtime* and for the serious mind, *The Brains Trust*.

When the American Forces Network was established British listeners were treated to the big band sounds of Glenn Miller and Tommy Dorsey, jazz concerts by Benny Carter, the singing talents of Ella FitzGerald and a new singing phenomenon named Frank Sinatra. American comedians like Bob Hope, Jack Benny and Red Skelton also proved popular.

Cinemas and theatres throughout the country were closed on the declaration of war for fear of imminent air attack but within a few weeks they had all reopened.

League football was without doubt the biggest crowd puller of the 1930s. On Saturday 2 September 1939, over 370,000 fans had watched League football games despite travelling difficulties.

There was trouble at Blackpool when a whiskey bottle was thrown at the Wolves goalkeeper but order was restored when the referee asked if two policemen could be sent for to patrol the crowd.

The Football League was abandoned and reorganised on a local basis. Grimsby Town played in the East Midlands Regional Division in 1939-40 along with Doncaster Rovers, Notts County, Chesterfield, Barnsley, Mansfield Town, Sheffield United, Sheffield Wednesday, Nottingham Forest, Rotherham United and Lincoln City. For the 1940-41 season, a second reorganisation produced the North Regional League giving Grimsby the chance to play against sides like Newcastle United, Middlesbrough, Burnley and Huddersfield Town.

The main problem facing League sides was that many of their players had been called up for duty with the armed forces. The problem was partly resolved with players 'guesting' for sides, though there were occasions when volunteers from the crowd were called for. One such game between Norwich City and Brighton & Hove Albion saw Brighton field a team which included five of their own players, two Norwich reserves and four soldiers. Norwich won 18-0.

Sports facilities were provided at most public parks. The hire of a tennis court cost 6d per hour for grass, 1/6 for a hard court. Bowls cost 4d per player per hour and pitch-and-putt on an eighteen hole course cost 9d per player per round. Other popular pastimes included cycling and walking.

SATURDAY TELEGRAPH
FOOTBALL ANNUAL
NOW ON SALE

FOR FULL DETAILS AND FIXTURES OF ALL THE LOCAL CLUBS

PACKED WITH UP-TO-DATE INFORMATION

GRIMSBY A.R.P.

CARRY YOUR GAS MASK

The "Telegraph" is asked by the Town Clerk, Mr. L. W. Heeler, to say that shopkeepers must obscure all external lighting and reduce lighting as much as possible.

Motorists must not use headlights but drive with side lamps only.

All householders must take measures to prevent light being visible from the outside of their home.

Gas masks should be carried by everybody wherever they go.

DRUM-HEAD SERVICE CANCELLED

Owing to the present situation the Chief Constable of Grimsby, informs the " Telegraph " that he is unable to take the risk of allowing a large number of people to gather in one place.

It is therefore with regret that the Drum-head Service, which was to have been held in the People's Park on Sunday has been cancelled.

HAVE WATER READY

The Chief Constable states that it is desirable that householders should keep the bath or other receptacles filled with water for the purpose of dealing with possible fires. Those people who can do so are advised to purchase a Home Office stirrup pump, for dealing with incendiary bombs.

RAID SIGNALS

Warning of impending air raids will be given by a fluctuating or "warbling" signal of varying pitch, or a succession of intermittent blasts, sounded by hooters and sirens.

These signals may be supplemented by sharp blasts on Police whistles.

The " Raiders Passed " signal will be a continuous signal at a steady pitch.

If Poison Gas has been used, warning will be given by Hand Rattles. The ringing of Hand Bells will announce that the danger from gas has passed.

25. Gas mask drill for the young.

An ARP ambulance. Just visible in the background is part of the ornamental cast-iron entrance to the People's Park. The structure did not survive the war; it was demolished in January 1943 during one of the salvage campaigns and melted down.

27-28. *Above:* The Grimsby ARP mobile column photographed in Park Drive during an exercise. The lead vehicle is a conver
bus. *Below:* Ambulances ready for the off. The photograph was taken in 1941 at the old Cattle Market in Cromwell Roa

UNIFORM FOR ALL A.R.P. WORKERS

SIR JOHN ANDERSON, the Home Secretary, announced in the House of Commons yesterday that all A.R.P. workers are to be given a uniform.

It would cost about 11s. per person, and would be a utility [gar]ment, like an overall, to cover [ord]inary clothes.

[I]t is not anticipated that supplies [wil]l be ready in quantity for some [we]eks. The uniform will be dark blue [wit]h a red badge and the letters A.R.P. [on] the left breast.

[D]uring a long speech, Sir John [rev]ealed that there were to be no [wh]olesale sackings of full-time A.R.P. [per]sonnel, but local authorities were [bei]ng asked to arrange for a nucleus [sta]nd-by force which could be sup[ple]mented by other volunteers.

FIRST-LINE UNITS

[T]here would be certain reductions [in] stand-by forces, but the scope of [th]em would not be known until local [aut]horities had completed their [rev]iews.

[I]t was not proposed, however, that [on] the new basis, first-line units which [con]tained a substantial number of [wh]ole-time workers should be more [th]an 50 per cent. of the total strength. [Th]at arrangement assumed that [me]ans would be made so that the

second line could come quickly into action.

In some areas, he anticipated that an increase in personnel would be necessary.

Report of Speech, Page Five

More Butter For Germans

Germans are to have their butter ration almost doubled, the German news agency stated yesterday. The announcement adds that the new ration will be given under ration cards covering the period from October 23 to November 19.

Children up to six years of age will also receive a double portion of butter.

The Berlin correspondent of the "Berlingske Tidende." of Copenhagen, recently gave the German butter ration as three ounces per head a week.

Women doing MANUAL LABOUR for their COUNTRY

—can still keep their hands lovely

Women who do rough mechanics' work in the ambulance corps, land girls, fire fighters and W.A.T.'s find that they can still keep their hands smooth and lovely, if they have a supply of 'Vaseline' Petroleum Jelly in their kit.

known. *Always make sure that the surface of the skin is thoroughly clean and non-septic BEFORE applying 'Vaseline' Jelly.*

1 **FOR HANDS UNACCUSTOMED TO ROUGH WORK.** Rub 'Vaseline' Jelly well into your hands *every night*, then wipe off. This keeps the skin pliable, prevents blisters, hard patches and cracks.

2 **FOR SORE FEET.** There's nothing like 'Vaseline' Jelly for preventing blisters or sores from heavy boots or extra strain on your feet. Massage feet well frequently.

3 **FOR CUTS AND BRUISES.** 'Vaseline' Jelly is the best emollient and protective covering

Vaseline
TRADE MARK
Petroleum Jelly

Chesebrough Manufacturing Co. Cons'd.,
Victoria Road, London, N.W.10

4287-8

30. *Below:* ARP rescue exercise.

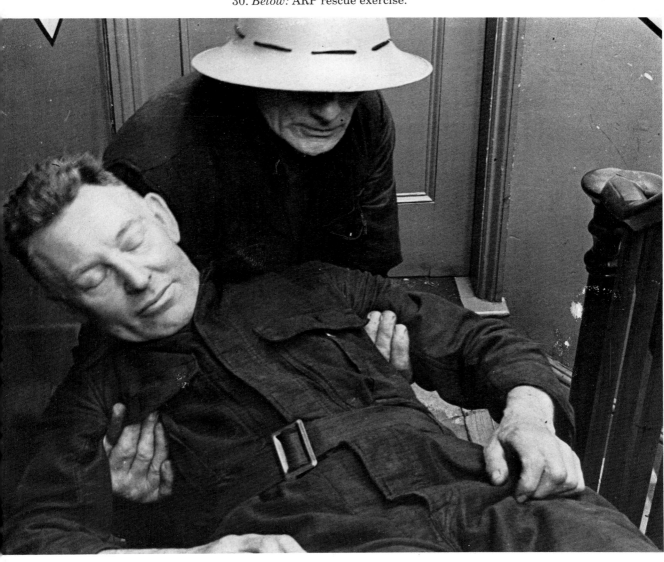

IN THE EVENT OF AN AIR-RAID...

ARE **YOU** FULLY PREPARED?

BLACKOUT MATERIAL IN STOCK

54in. Black Italian Cloth   2 9 per yd.
30in. Black Twill Lining   1 3 per yd.
54in. Bolton Twill in
Black, Blue and Brown   2 11 per yd.
50in. Green Lining ......   1 11 per yd.

BLIND MATERIAL

X-Ray Cloth, completely light proof, 60in. x 72i
Greyfriars Paper Blinds made ready to hand, ca
    be bought by the yard in 52in. and 58in. width
    at 3d. per sq. ft.
50in. Blind material, completely light proof,
    Black, Green, and Brown.
Plenty of Navy Blue and Holland Blind.

32. Is this the penalty for being late on parade? Not quite — it's an ARP rescue drill. Even a passing cat has to admire th handywork of the wardens — and the courage of the 'victim'.

34-35. Senior personel attending ARP exercise.

36. The Mayor of Cleethorpes, Alderman Croft Bak[er] presenting a cup to A Watch, Headquarters Section of [the] AFS, who won a firefighting competition at Blundell Pa[rk.] The team included Leading Fireman E Haith, Firema[n] Machon, Fireman S Spir and Fireman A E Skelton. Dep[uty] Chief Officer J Gray is also in the picture.

NEW LIVES · NEW NEEDS

CINEMA USHER
becomes A.F.S. HERO
(braver than any film one)

Last year you saw him marshalling the film queues — tall, white-gloved, immaculate. Now the gloves are off all right! He's in the A.F.S., and night after night he answers the call of danger. What an abrupt, dramatic change — and what a tremendous toll it has taken of his nerves and stamina.

THE EVER WELCOME CUP

Solace and satisfaction are always to be found in a cup of really good tea. Get them in full measure by insisting on

MAZAWATTEE
The Quality TEA

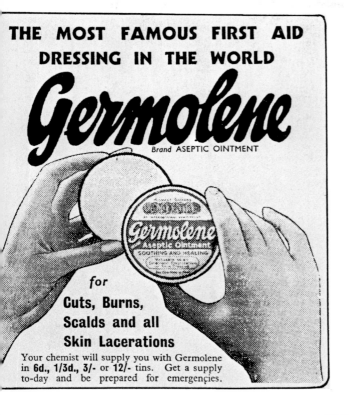

THE MOST FAMOUS FIRST AID DRESSING IN THE WORLD

Germolene

Brand ASEPTIC OINTMENT

for

Cuts, Burns, Scalds and all Skin Lacerations

Your chemist will supply you with Germolene in 6d., 1/3d., 3/- or 12/- tins. Get a supply to-day and be prepared for emergencies.

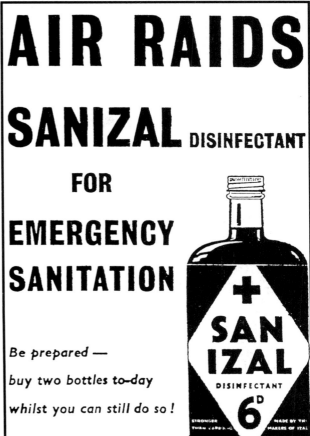

AIR RAIDS

SANIZAL DISINFECTANT

FOR

EMERGENCY

SANITATION

Be prepared —

buy two bottles to-day

whilst you can still do so !

Newton, Chambers & Co. Ltd., Thorncliffe, nr. Sheffield

SAN IZAL DISINFECTANT 6ᴰ

40. Nurses line up to welcome the Duchess of Gloucester during her visit to Grimsby General Hospital.

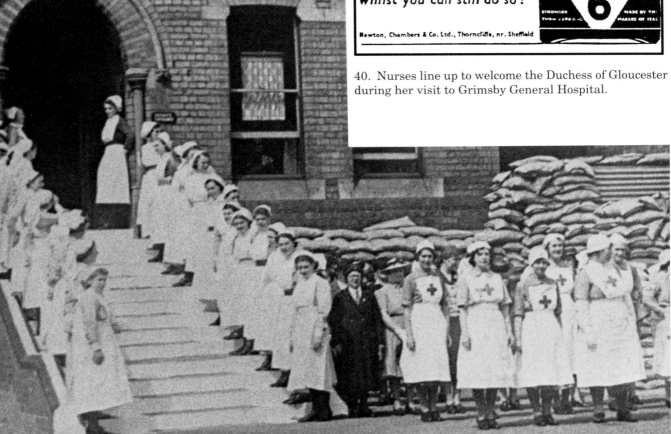

42 *Above*. ARP first aid party, old Scartho Road Hospital, 1941.

43 *Below* ARP wedding, 1 August 1941. The Guard of Honour sport new battledress uniforms as Tom and Madge Elliott leave St Luke's Church, Grimsby.

The Home Guard

[O]peration Dynamo was a success and altogether [6],427 British and Allied servicemen and women had [be]en evacuated from the Continent via the Dunkirk [be]aches and a number of French ports.

[In] the minds of everyone in these islands was one [wo]rd: INVASION. The Rt Hon Anthony Eden, Minister [of] State for War, planned the raising of Local Defence [Vo]lunteers (LDV) to augment the regular troops; he [br]oadcast an immediate appeal for civilian men be[tw]een the ages of 17 and 65 to report, without delay, to [the]ir local police stations for vetting (to weed out po[ten]tial Fifth Columnists), although no medical exami[na]tion was required.

[Th]e first LDVs were provided with a stencilled arm[ba]nd, a whistle and a pike-shaft or broom-handle, [tho]ugh some did carry their own sporting guns. It was [no]t until August 1940 that uniforms were supplied and [Ch]urchill, having his own way, renamed this civilian [ar]my The Home Guard.

[By] May 1941 some 1,600,000 volunteers had enrolled, [an]d, more importantly, they were adequately armed. [Gr]adually more sophisticated weapons came along — [Ste]n guns, sticky-bombs, Blacker Bombards, Northover [Pr]ojectors, and the superb Browning Automatic Rifle. [Ch]urchill urged that the Home Guard be allowed to [ma]n anti-aircraft guns and heavy searchlights. At last [th]e 'Look, Duck and Vanish' image of the early cynics [fa]ded.

[La]te in 1944 the Home Guard, tried and found true, bat[te]red in many cases by air-raids, was finally stood [do]wn. Note that phrase. It was not disbanded; the men [we]re not demobilised. Are they therefore, technically, [sti]ll serving?

[Th]ose who served in the Home Guard were entitled to [th]e Defence Medal.

Mr ASHBY leads a 'double' life!

1. You'd think Mr. Ashby, who works twice as hard now that half his office staff is gone, would call it a day when he puts his key in his front door. But

3. . . . he's fit and fresh for his Home Guard training ; and it does his heart good to know he can " go to it " like a youngster!

2. . . . as soon as he gets in he takes a Lifebuoy Toilet Soap bath! That quickly gets rid of sticky perspiration. So that . . .

THE hustle of these busy days makes it more than ever necessary to keep fit and fresh. Lifebuoy Toilet Soap, with its deep-cleansing lather, quickly washes away all stale perspiration—keeps you feeling fresh, active, and invigorated.

LIFEBUOY TOILET SOAP
Refreshes, Invigorates, Prevents "B.O."

4D PER TABLET (INCLUDES PURCHASE TAX)

LBT 545-836-55

— A *LEVER* PRODUCT

45. Photo-call for members of the Lindsey Battalion, Home Guard, at the Toll Bar School, New Waltham, 1 October 1944. The units commanding officer of the unit was Major H S Bloomer.

THE BOOMPS

"He says he just couldn't bear to be separated from his . . ."

46. Initially, the Home Guard was equipped with weapons supplied from the USA, including Tommy guns. These particular weapons had been made famous — or infamous — by American gangsters who christened them *Chicago Typewriters*.

47. They went that way! A light-hearted moment from men of Goxhill Home Guard.

48. Augusta Street Barracks, late 1943 or early 1944. This unit was drawn from Grimsby and Scartho.

49. Fulstow and Marshchapel platoon whose task was to patrol and defend the coastline between North Cotes and Grainthorpe Haven.

50. Some of the members of Cleethorpes Home Guard. Their headquarters was in High Street where the old Woolworths was situated.

The Blitz

As a fishing port Grimsby escaped relatively lightly from the attentions of the *Luftwaffe* when compared to the damage and destruction inflicted upon Hull, Cardiff, Liverpool, Southampton, Swansea and Clydebank. The majority of raids against the town were undertaken by single aircraft, indicating that Grimsby was one of those targets often selected by the Germans for the propaganda value of announcing the attack; any damage inflicted was a bonus.

To the end of November 1941, the pattern of raids on Grimsby was similar to other fishing ports. Grimsby had endured 22 raids resulting in 1,700 houses being damaged and 18 civilians killed, whilst Fraserburgh had had 17 raids with 700 houses damaged and 40 civilians killed. Aberdeen had had 24 raids leaving 2,000 houses damaged and 68 civilians dead, and Lowestoft had been bombed 53 times resulting in 9,000 houses damaged and 94 people killed.

Grimsby's first sighting of the enemy occurred on 29 October 1939 when a Heinkel flew over the town on what was probably a reconnaissance mission, but it was not until 22 June 1940 that the first bombs fell when fields at Love Lane Corner were straddled.

The attacks continued; on 6 September a lone raider scattered incendiaries across the town and in December there were five attacks. Four bombs were dropped on houses in Heneage Road. A lone raider was sighted by a Blenheim over Mansfield and bombs later fell near Grimsby and also at Grantham and Mabelthorpe. Four nights fighter-bombers attacked Scampton airfield and one of the raiders, after shooting down a Hampden, went on to bomb Lincoln and Grimsby from only 150 feet.

In February 1941 bombs fell in Grimsby, where houses in Arlington Street and Lord Street suffered direct hits; the public library was also destroyed. A few days later bombs fell in Rosevere Avenue and in February serious damage was done to the West Marsh sidings.

Thursday 27 February 1941 has since become known as *Bloody Thursday*; others remember it as the day they bombed the Oberon. The raid lasted only a few minutes and was carried out by a solitary Dornier Do 127. It was a classic tip-and-run raid designed more to test the nerve of the local population than to cause any material damage — that was a bonus. The Dornier emerged from low cloud over Humberston and raked Waltham Toll Bar School with its machine gun. Another burst of gunfire narrowly missed a No 8 bus in Humberston Avenue.

The raider then turned, swung over Cleethorpes and turned to attack Grimsby — the result was devastating. The stick of bombs dropped by the raider plus the machine gun fire which raked the length of Cleethorpe Road killed eleven people and seriously wounded another twenty seven. As the Dornier headed towards the coast the aircraft machine gunned traffic in Scartho Road and Louth Road.

In human terms it was one of the worst days of the war for Grimsby. Among the casualties were two children, killed on their way back to school. Others died when the Oberon, the dockers' pub, collapsed as a bomb hit an adjoining fruit shop.

Of the raids that did take place, only two were of major significance. There was the attack which became known as the butterfly bomb raid on the night of 13-14 June 1943, when 99 people were killed. A month later 64 died when around 30 tonnes of high explosives were dropped on the town.

Grimsby and Plymouth jointly hold the unique but dubious distinction of being the only places in Great Britain where anti-personnel butterfly bombs were dropped, causing the maximum amount of disruption both during a raid and after. And for the Germans it worked brilliantly, only thanks to tight security they never found out just how successful they had been. Large areas of Grimsby and Cleethorpes were paralysed by the threat, real or otherwise, from these devices. Being comparatively small, butterfly bombs were still being discovered long after the war was over and claimed their last victim in 1945, more than two years after the night they had been dropped.

On 13 July Grimsby suffered major damage. Though no butterfly bombs were dropped, 30 tonnes of high explosives destroyed or badly damaged many of the town's famous buildings including St James' Church, the Tivoli, All Saints Church and the Strand Cinema. Bombs also fell in Algernon Street, Doughty Road, Abbey Walk, Garden Street, Duchess Street, Vaughan Avenue, Dudley Street, Heneage Road, Freeman Street, Albion Street, Bath Street, Guildford Street, Harold Street, Castle Street, Crescent Street, Lord Street, Anderson Street, Fildes Street, South Parade, the Fish Docks, Riby Street, New Clee Sidings, Harrington Street, Carr Lane, Grimsby Road, Brereton Avenue, Daubney Street, Sidney Street, Frankland Place, Pendreth Place and Wintringham's woodyard.

The last attack occurred on 4 March 1945 when houses in Grimsby, Cleethorpes and Humberston were raked with machine gun fire.

51. Anderson shelters under construction.

52-53. The remains of Grimsby's old public library in Burgess Street after it took a direct hit during a raid in February 1941.

FIRE GUARDS get ready!
FIREBOMB FRITZ is coming

Men and women of Britain's Fire Guard *will* be ready. Ready because during quiet times we train and practise, every day learning to do our job better. We're not asking for trouble, but we'll meet it properly when it does come.

FIRE GUARD TIPS.
No. 9 Don't enter a burning building or room unless you have something to attack the fire with.
No. 9 Keep all doors and windows shut at night as far as possible. Fire thrives on draughts or fresh air.
10 If a burning room gets too hot for you, shut the door as you retreat. It cuts off the air supply. Besides, a door is a good fire stop.

BURN BRITAIN

BRITAIN SHALL NOT BURN!

ISSUED BY THE MINISTRY OF HOME SECURITY

55. *Above right:* 30 May 1942. One of the raiders attacking Hull dropped its payload of incendiaries by mistake on the village of Barrow-on-Humber. The resulting fires attracted another plane which dropped a stick of high-explosive bombs across the village.

56. Grimsby Police Auxiliary Messengers pictured in 1943. With them are Inspectors Duricott and Holland. The job of the messengers was to keep communications open during air raids, when it was expected that telephone cables would be damaged by the bombing. During the raid of 13 July 1943, the police post in Harold Street was flattened by blast when a bomb landed on the house next door.

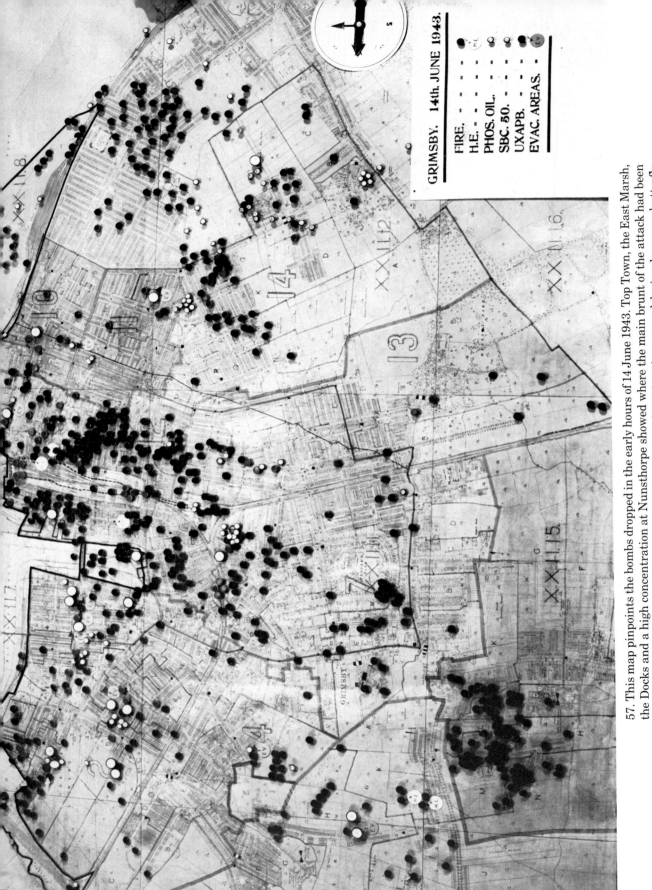

GRIMSBY. 14th. JUNE 1943.

FIRE.   - - - -
H.E.   - - - -
PHOS. OIL. - - - -
SBC. 50.   - - - -
UXAPB.   - - - -
EVAC. AREAS. -

57. This map pinpoints the bombs dropped in the early hours of 14 June 1943. Top Town, the East Marsh, the Docks and a high concentration at Nunsthorpe showed where the main brunt of the attack had been felt. It was the raid in which the *Luftwaffe* dropped around 3,000 anti-personnel devices known as butterfly bombs.

58. Small but extremely deadly — a butterfly bomb

59. Charlie Heath was one of those who made the ultimate sacrifice. On duty the night the butterfly bombs fell, Charlie and his son Walter were on ARP duty, and, with George Wilson and Harold Blundell, they went to investigate an object dropped on Canon Ainslie School. One of them is believed to have touched it and Germany's newest terror weapon claimed four more lives.

60. It's 1947 but the search continues for butterfly bombs. Here, German prisoners of war sweep the old cemetery, Grimsby.

61. If the butterfly bomb raid claimed the most casualties, it was the raid a month later which did the most damage when more than thirty tonnes of high explosive were dropped across the town. This is the remains of Sanders Maltings.

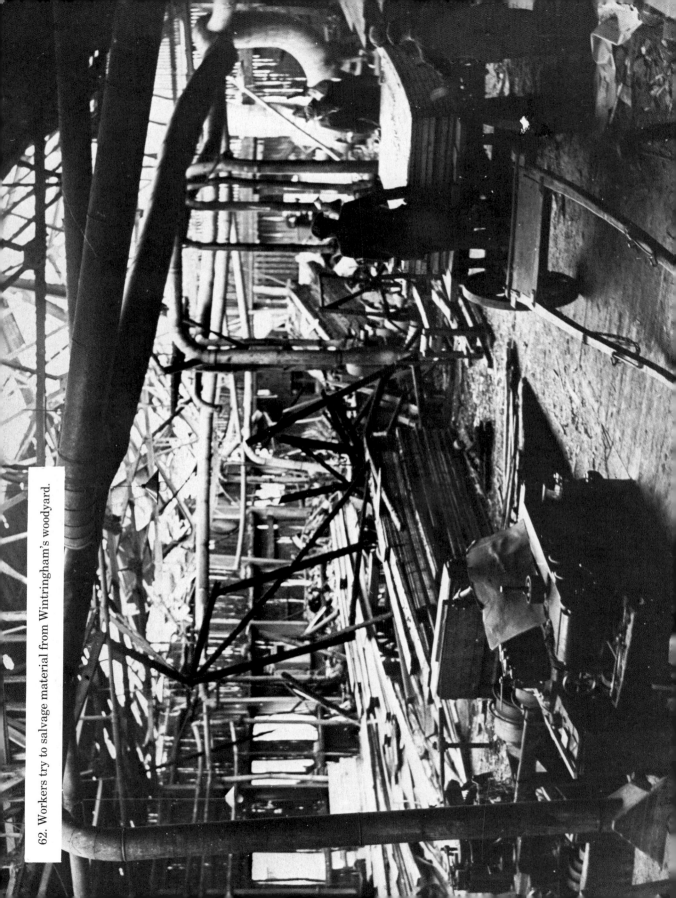

62. Workers try to salvage material from Wintringham's woodyard.

63. A huge crater tore the road and the surrounding houses were destroyed by the blast.

64. An unidentified area of the town wrecked by a high explosive bomb.

65. The remains of the Bon Marche, Lawson & Stockdale shop, on Cleethorpe Road, Grimsby.

66. The remains of the Pontoon on Grimsby Fish Docks.

67. The Duchess Street area.

AIR RAID
DAMAGE

JAYS

Furniture
Replacement
Scheme

IMMEDIATE HELP

3 YEARS to PAY

DELIVERY on FIRST agreed PAYMENT

Still available, splendid assortment of Bedroom suites, Three-piece suites and Dining-room suites. From 10/- MONTHLY

JAYS FURNISHING STORES

Write or call for particulars

248, 249, 250, TOTTENHAM COURT RD., W.1
TELEPHONE: MUSEUM 8255 and 8256.   (OXFORD STREET END)
MANCHESTER, 1 . . . . 26-28-30, Oldham Street
BIRMINGHAM, 5 . . . . . 99-101, Bristol Street
LIVERPOOL . . . . . . 58-60-62, Church Street
EDINBURGH . . . . . . 39-40-41, Princes Street
LEEDS . . . . 85, New Briggate
GLASGOW, C.2 . . . . . . 19-25, Sauchiehall Street
170 OTHER BRANCHES

PLACE A (X) AGAINST THOSE REQUIRED

FREE	SUPER CATALOGUE — Post Free	
	Please ask your representative to call with photographs and patterns.	
	Please send details of your scheme of IMMEDIATE HELP in cases where goods to be purchased from you are damaged or destroyed by bombs.	

NAME

AIR RAID PRECAUTIONS
—
MESSENGERS URGENTLY
NEEDED in Rural Districts
—
Will MOTOR-CYCLISTS and Owners of Light Cars offer their services WITHOUT DELAY to the Grimsby Rural District Council

Deansgate, Grimsby.

71. St James's Church. Publication of this photograph was banned until August 1943.

72. All Saints' Heneage Road.

73-74. Not all the raiders returned home.

FOR EMERGENCY
SANITATION

SANIZAL

SAN IZAL DISINFECTANT

6ᵈ

SANIZAL

77. *Below:* Grimsby air-raid wardens who volunteered for a three-week tour of duty in London at the height of the V1 rocket attacks. They are pictured at Grimsby Town station before boarding a train for the capital.

78. Crewmen prepare a twin Lewis gun for firing.

Trawlers at War

Grimsby's fishing fleet fought the war on two fronts. Firstly, there were those vessels which remained to carry on the tasks of commercial fishing; secondly, there were those — and sometimes their crews — which were requisitioned by the Admiralty for service with the Royal Navy as auxiliary patrol vessels or minesweepers. Whether catching cod or sweeping mines, hunting for fish or hunting for U-boats, dodging the weather or dodging bombs, Grimsby's trawlermen played a vital part in the nation's war effort.

It was on 28 October 1938 that Grimsby's first casualty of the war occurred when the *Lynx II* was sunk by a U-boat ninety miles off Scotland. Over the next six years the *Grimsby Evening Telegraph* would report another 119 fishing boats from the port as war losses.

Some trawlers were able to bite back! The Strath class trawler *Chandos* (GY1290) had been requisitioned by the Admiralty in November 1939 as an auxiliary patrol vessel but was returned for commercial fishing in January 1940. On 31 March 1940 she was attacked by a German plane whilst making for the North Sea fishing grounds through a snow squall. The first burst of machine gun fire hit the wheelhouse killing skipper John Upton instantly. Trimmer Clifford Rawlins (18 years old), though himself badly wounded, managed to make his way to the trawler's Lewis gun and opened fire upon the attacker. As the plane came in for its third pass, Rawlins succeeded in hitting the aircraft in the tail. As smoke began to trail behind the aircraft it turned for home and disappeared. Later, wreckage of a German plane was trawled up in *Chandos'* nets. Clifford Rawlins was later awarded the BEM and the Lloyds War Medal for bravery.

Grimsby vessels lost include: *Lynx II, Wigmore, Pearl, Resercho, Croxton, Leonora, Penn, Hercules II, Slasher, Greynight, Volante, Salacon, Northwards, Mistletoe, Pride, Carlton, Windsor, Robinia, Rodney, Joan Margaret, Elmira, Alaskan, Kimberley, Ontario, Fortuna, Sylvia, King Erik, Ophir II, The Tetrarch, Manx Admiral, Lord Shrewsbury, Parthian, William Hanbury, Rononia, Bromelia, Bombay, Pride of the Humber, Leo, Elsie, Premier, Sally Ann, Retriever, Chancellor, Iranian, Emerald, Aquarious, Falmouth, Dinorah.* Grimsby vessels lost whilst on Admiralty service include: *Washington, Rutlandshire*, Bradman, Hammond*, Athelstan, Larwood, Jardine, Calvi, Argyllshire, Blackburn Rovers, Sisapon, Murmansk, Lapwing II, Castleton, Campina, Rodino, Staunton, Drummer, Oswaldian, Resparko, Royalo, Sea King, Resolvo, Rinovia, William Wesney, Ristango, Arsenal, Fontenoy, Kennymore, Manx Prince, Calverton, Capricornus, Cortina, Refundo, Gadra, Desiree, Relonzo, Luda Lady, Darogah, Arctic Trapper, Ormonde, Lincoln City, Benvolio, Remillo, Gullfoss, Earl Essex, Lord Selbourne, Barham* (drifter), *Othello, Kopanes, Alberic, Susarian, Silicia, Resmilo, Akranes, Lorinda, Nubia, Emilion, Notts County, Solomon, Tunisian, Heron, Waterfly, Leyland, Moravia, Franc Tireur, Meror, Wyoming.* Trawlers marked* were salvaged and used by either the Germans or in the Faroes or Norway.

Below: A trawler under attack.

80. A raider's eye view of a trawler. This photograph was taken from a German plane operating over the North Sea.

81. A Mello turns to attack a trawler. The first Grimsby trawler lost to air attack was the *Pearl* which was bombed and sunk 65 miles from the mouth of the Humber. One of her crew died in the attack and two others were wounded. Also attacked by the same raider but not hit were the *Proheus, Sheldon* and *Remillo*. On 31 January 1940, the *Russell* was bombed and machine-gunned by a lone raider. Her crew took to the boats, but after the raider had left, returned and managed to bring the damaged vessel back to port.

82. A trawlerman takes cover as his ship is strafed by a raider.

83. The *Rigoletto* was strafed by a raider on 29 January 1940, her skipper and the mate were both killed.

84. The *Etruria* was bombed off Scotland but managed to reach Aberdeen. Three of her crew died in the attack.

85. Running the gauntlet. A trawler on escort duty and her charge come under attack.

86-87. In the early months of the war trawlers were pressed into Admiralty service as auxiliary patrol vessels, and assigned to contraband control duties. Their task was to intercept and search neutral merchantships and to confiscate any cargo thought to be destined for the Nazi war effort. In these photographs, the patrol has boarded a merchantship and identified a cargo of wolfram (ore used in steel manufacture) as a contraband. In the first two months of the war 289,000 tonnes of goods were confiscated.

88-89. HMT *Cambridgeshire* was requisitioned by the *Admiralty* in August 1939 for anti-submarine duties. Transferred to Swansea, *Cambridgeshire* took part in the evacuation of the British Expeditionary Force from France, one of her tasks being to bring General Sir Alan Brooke (*centre*), his general staff and a number of French officers, out of St Nazaire and back to Britain. The young man in the singlet in the photograph below is George Beasley, the chief engineer, who, with skipper Billy Euston, came from Grimsby.

90-91. A dramatic moment in the career of HMT *Cambridgeshire* as she comes to the aid of the stricken liner *Lancastria*, bombed off the French coast in June 1940. *Cambridgeshire* picked up 1,009 survivors but another 4,000 troops and Air Force personnel went down with the ship.

92. A group of former Grimsby fishermen pose for an unknown cameraman on a South Coast beach after taking part in the successful operation to lift more than 300,000 men from the beaches around Dunkirk.

93. During the war large numbers of trawlers and drifters were requisitioned for Admiralty service, performing a wide range of tasks from minesweeping, anti-submarine and auxiliary patrol duties, to less glamorous but equally important duties as fleet tenders.

94. HMT *Leicester City* spent part of the war patrolling between Scapa Flow and Thorshaven in the Faroes, and during one trip she sank a U-boat.

95. Built in 1938 and requisitioned in September 1939 for anti-submarine duties, HMT *Ayrshire* was returned for commercial fishing in October 1945.

96. HMT *Northern Gem*, one of fifteen sisterships requisitioned by the Admiralty. The 655 tonne vessels were built in Germany in 1936 and caused something of a stir when they first arrived at Grimsby. Not only were they bigger than other Grimsby based trawlers but they also offered a standard of crew accommodation superior to that of their contemporaries. Some of these ships served on convoy rescue or as armed boarding vessels prior to conversion to the anti-submarine role. Five of the class were transferred to the United States Navy in 1942, and, with the exception of *Northern Princess* which was lost on 7 March 1942, were returned in early 1946.

97. Stand easy for crew members of HMT *Northern Gem*.

98. Officers of HMT *Northern Gem. Left to right:* Lieutenant W King RNR of Yarmouth, J Pooley of Fleetwood, W Gatt of Aberdeen and A Hodson of Grimsby.

99. HMT *Northern Pride* on winter convoy duty. Photograph issued 1945.

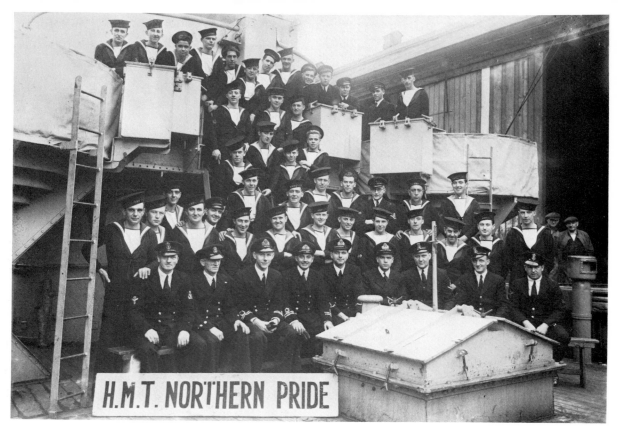

H.M.T. NORTHERN PRIDE

100-101. *Above:* HMT *Northern Pride. Below:* HMT *Northern Sky*

102 & 104. HMT *Northern Sky* on patrol.

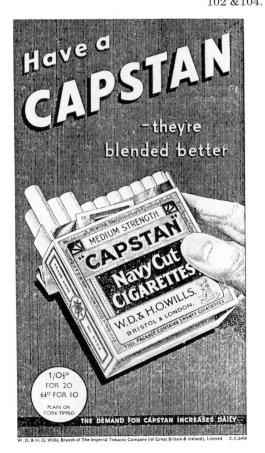

Have a **CAPSTAN**

– they're blended better

MEDIUM STRENGTH
CAPSTAN
Navy Cut
CIGARETTES

W. D. & H. O. WILLS,
BRISTOL & LONDON.

THIS PACKAGE CONTAINS TWENTY CIGARETTES

1/0½D
FOR 20
6½D FOR 10
PLAIN OR
CORK TIPPED

THE DEMAND FOR CAPSTAN INCREASES DAILY

W. D. & H. O. Wills, Branch of The Imperial Tobacco Company (of Great Britain & Ireland), Limited   C.C.641B

105. Auxiliary patrol operations room, Grimsby.

106. A visit from the chaplain.

107. One of five sisterships built by the Great Central Railway for the North Sea routes, SS *Bury* was launched in November 1910 and cost £41,500 to build. Transferred to Associated Humber Lines in 1935, *Bury* ran the last return trip to Hamburg just days before the start of World War II, arriving back at Grimsby on 25 August. Towards the end of 1941 *Bury* and her sisters were converted to convoy rescue ships. This involved fitting extra accommodation and sick bay facilities as well as a large number of life rafts. Based on the Clyde they accompanied convoys across the Atlantic saving hundreds of lives, though one ship, *Stockport*, was lost with all hands and survivors from the *Eastern Trader* from when she was torpedoed by **V604** on 23 February 1943.

108. HMS *Grimsby* was an escort sloop displacing 990 tonnes and launched at Devonport on 19 July 1933. She was the name ship of a class of thirteen vessels including four built for the Royal Australian Navy (*Yarra, Swan, Parramatta* and *Warrego*) and one for the Royal Indian Navy (*Indus*).

109. Painting by Rowland Langmaid of HMS *Grimsby* and the South African whaler *Southern Maid* escorting the tanker *Helka* to Tobruk.

HMS Grimsby

During the grim week following the retreat in Greece, the loss of Crete and the German advance across North Africa towards Egypt and the Suez Canal, the isolated fortress of Tobruk held out and came under a siege that was to last for 242 days. That Tobruk held out for so long was due both the determination of the defending garrison and the Royal Navy whose main task was to bring in supplies of stores, food, petrol and ammunition.

On 25 May 1941, HMS *Grimsby* and the South African armed whaler *Southern Maid*, were en route to Tobruk escorting the SS *Helka* which was carrying a cargo of petrol and water, when they were attacked by Stuka dive-bombers. Bombs were dropped near the *Helka* and *Grimsby* and the *Southern Maid* was machine-gunned though she in turn hit two of her attackers.

Two hours later, the *Luftwaffe* returned. The *Helka* was hit by two bombs and broke in half. The aft section of the ship (where the engines were) continued to sail on. The forepart remained afloat with most of the crew clinging to it. Having stopped the engines, boats were lowered and the crew rescued.

The *Grimsby* shot down two aircraft before she too was bombed and sunk. All this time the *Southern Maid* put up an intense anti-aircraft barrage and succeeded in bringing down one aircraft and damaging several others. When the *Luftwaffe* withdrew she picked up the survivors and made for Mersa Matruh. *Right: Grimsby,* having been hit, begins to settle in the water. *Below: Grimsby* is down by the stern. On the right in the background is the bow section of the *Helka*.

112. The destroyer HMS *Scorpion* leads a sub-division of the 23rd Flotilla round the Humber Lightship.

113. Saturday night at New Waltham Royal Naval Wireless Station. This photograph was taken in February 1943 and shows staff at the station together with wives and friends at one of the regular social nights held in the canteen.

114. Haile and Bull Sands forts, off Grimsby, were under the control of Northern Command and manned by 274 and 275 Batteries of the 513th Coast Regiment, Royal Artillery. The photograph was taken on 11 February 1942 by Lieutenant O'Brien.

115. A gun crew at action stations, 11 February 1942.

116. Soldiers in hammocks. As can be seen the accommodation on the forts had a Spartan flavour about it, and life could be monotonous especially when heavy weather cut links with the mainland.

117. Conways of Cleethorpes to the rescue!

119. With the British Expeditionary Force (BEF). The CO of the 2nd Battalion Lincolnshire Regiment at his headquarters in the St Pol area during a divisional exercise. The 2nd Lincolns formed part of the 9th Infantry Brigade, 3rd Division, II Corps.

120. Anti-tank crew of the 2nd Lincolns, St Pol area.

" NOW! WHERE'S THAT BLOKE HITLER !! "

"REPAIR SQUAD, PLEASE!"

Yesterday . . . in the garage . . . repairing cars . . . "a little trouble with the plugs, sir ? Soon get that fixed !" Today a soldier—right in the thick of it . . . shells bursting . . . snipers taking a crack at him. But he does it ! And repairs another tank—ready for action ! Salute his toughness—his endurance ! Salute the Soldier — with more savings ! Let us all vow to-day to mobilize our money—by cutting spending and increasing lending. Let us lend to our country—and so lend practical help "to the boys out there!"

SALUTE THE SOLDIER

123. 2nd Lincolns at Ross-on-Wye, August 1940.

124. Camouflaged section post of the 8th Lincolns.

125. November 1940 and Lieutenant-General Sir Ronald Adam, GOC Northern Command, watches the results of firing from a pillbox at Mabelthorpe where the 7th Lincolns were on coast defence duties.

126. Evacuation from Namsos during the Norwegian Campaign, April 1940. Men of the 4th Lincolns man a road-block on the outskirts of Skagge.

127. Writing home. A soldier of the 4th Lincolns at Skagge.

128. September 1944 and troops of the 6th Lincolns, 138 Brigade, 46th Division, have advanced into the centre of the Gothic Line. In this photograph a Bren carrier passes over a small bridge during the advance. In the background is a German barrack block.

129. This dug-in tank turret was held by a light machine gun troop, which withdrew their gun in good order only after coming under heavy attack from our forces. The Churchill tank in the background has hit a mine and lost a track.

130. Captured Japanese 37mm anti-tank gun. *Left to right:* Sergeant R Holgate, Company Sergeant Major B F Carter and Private H Taylor, all of the Lincolnshire Regiment.

1. Admiral Lord Louis Mountbatten, on his arrival at Palambang, Java, here he inspected a Guard of Honour formed by men of the 1st Battalion, ncolnshire Regiment.

AIR MAIL—PAR AVION

Dear Hawkins :

Last time I was Home on leave you expressed a wish to accompany me as batman " if the necessary strings could be manipulated, as it were ". Unfortunately, they couldn't, and my frugal wants are ministered to by a batman who was, in private life, a professional strong man in a circus. A most excellent man, but lacking both flair and temperament for making a really capable valet.

Will you believe it, Hawkins, when I tell you that he'd never heard of Rose's Lime Juice, and actually thought that a hangover was a term used by performers on the flying trapeze ? Needless to say, *that* gap in his education has already been made good.

We can get plenty of Rose's Lime Juice out here, but I doubt if it flows very plentifully at Home these days. Still, do lay in a few bottles if you can — they will come in handy for the victory celebrations !

Glad to hear you've got your three stripes in the H.G.

Best wishes,

Yours sincerely,

G. de St. G.

There is no substitute for ROSE'S Lime Juice

133-134. During their retreat across Holland, German forces destroyed dams and dykes causing flooding over vast stretches of the country and slowing the pace of the war. *Above:* 2nd Lincs patrol along the banks of the Maas. *Below:* Men of A Coy, 4th Lincolns, enter Willemstad, Holland.

135. Members of 385 detachment of the Territorial Army pose for an official photograph outside the Westward Ho Drill Hall, Grimsby, prior to their leaving their home town in the autumn of 1939 to take up duties with a searchlight battalion in the Tyneside area. They even took their own chefs with them!

136. Behind the wire . . . a group of prisoners pose for a photographer in a German POW camp. Most are wearing army uniform though one sports a sweater issued by the Shaw Saville Line. All nineteen are thought to have come from the Grimsby area. In 1944 a large number of prisoners were exchanged via neutral Sweden. One of the crew members of the ship used for the exchange was Fred Walker from Grimsby. The ship had just cleared Swedish waters on its return trip when the escorting German cruiser ordered it to stop. It appears that an escaped prisoner had managed to get on board and the Germans demanded that he be handed over otherwise everyone would have to get off the ship. The man eventually gave himself up and went over to the German cruiser in a small boat. The repatriation was then allowed to proceed.

137. Girls of the 2nd Lincs Platoon ATS — a unit drawn almost exclusively from Grimsby. In the early months of the war they were stationed at Doncaster where they provided meals for searchlight batteries across South Yorkshire and North Lincolnshire.

138. A line-up of cooks from Grimsby includes Violet Fowler, Marion Jacks, Letty Lawley and Margaret **Marshall**. The name of the girl on the extreme right is, alas, not known.

139. Hard at work in the cookhouse, the Grimsby ATS girls include Marion Jacks, Mary Cruddas, Margaret **Mussell** and Mary Brooks.

Keep Smiling
On "The Home Front"

Keep **fit** and enjoy radiant health this Winter with the aid of Bile Beans. Bile Beans tone up the system, purify the blood and daily remove all food residue. Thus Bile Beans improve your health, figure and complexion.

SOLD EVERYWHERE

Nightly

Bile Beans
BRAND PILLS

KEEP UP YOUR HEALTH & SPIRITS

60th Field Regiment

The 239th Field Battery of the 60th Field Regiment Royal Artillery was composed of 150 men from the Grimsby area. Equipped with 25-pounder guns, they were sent in as an anti-tank force during the fighting for Tobruk in November 1941.

Three days of vicious fighting later became known as the Battle of Sidi Rezegh, one of the most ferocious but least-known of the war. It was a battle in which many of the Grimsby men were killed, injured or taken prisoner.

The battle had its heroes including Brigadier Jock Campbell who, despite being wounded, took on the advancing panzers at point-blank range. Campbell led a squadron of tanks into battle in an open staff car. Later on he was manning one of the 60th Field Regiment's guns because the crews had taken heavy casualties. Campbell was awarded the VC — one of three won during the battle.

144. A 25-pounder field gun in action during an exercise "somewhere in England".

145-146. Heinkel 5J+KN, whilst en route to bomb RAF Leeming on the evening of 22 March 1941, entered the Humber balloon barrage where it came under fire from the 111th Light AA Battery, Gunner Dick Booth being credited with the Kill. The aircraft made a wheels-up landing in a field beside the Immingham-Habrough road. Two of the crew survived the crash.

EX-YEOMEN AND EX-CAVALRYMEN

WHO DESIRE TO SERVE TOGETHER
AS EX-SERVICEMEN SHOULD MEET
AT

CHANTRY HOUSE, BULL RING,

on MONDAY, SEPT. 4, at 8.0 p.m.

Organiser : ALEC HAXBY,

Lieutenant, Lincolnshire Yeomanry.

IF 50 PEOPLE DON'T TRAVEL

1 TANK CAN

At this most important time
Needless travel is a "crime"

BRITISH RAILWAYS

GWR — LMS — LNER — SR

UNITED TO WIN THE WAR

149. George Dring with his tank crew. Though from Grimsby, George saw service with the Sherwood Rangers Yeomanry who hold the distinction of being the first British troops to enter the Reich. On 24 September 1944, elements of the regiment crossed the German border at the village of Beek, four miles south-east of Nijmegen, as part of the armoured thrust that attempted to relieve the besieged paratroopers at Arnhem.

50. Members of Grimsby Civil Air Guard pictured at Waltham airfield a few weeks before the outbreak of the war. The Grimsby unit was formed in September 1938 as part of 25 Elementary & Reserve Flying Training School. Flying lessons were subsidised by the Government and, for as little as five shillings per hour, pilots could be trained on elementary machines. The men formed part of the RAFVR and many went on to distinguish themselves in both Fighter and Bomber Command.

51. This photograph shows almost a hundred members of the RAF Volunteer Reserve and was taken in Grimsby in the early days of the war. The RAFVR and the Auxiliary Air Force (AAF) were to prove their worth in the dark days to come. For example, on 15th September 1940, 504 (County of Nottingham) Squadron AAF was operating out of Hendon when they were scrambled to meet an aerial armada of approximately 150 German bombers. The squadron dived into a pack of Dornier DO17s of 1/KG76, which were approaching London. Flight Sergeant Ray Holmes racked one of the bombers from wing-tip to wing-tip. The Dornier began to disintegrate and plummeted onto the forecourt of Victoria Station. It is thought that this was the bomber which had attacked Buckingham Palace. In May 1940, 609 (West Riding) Squadron AAF moved south and helped provide air cover during the Dunkirk evacuation. In April 1942, the squadron re-equipped with Typhoon 1A fighters and in June 1944 was posted to Normandy providing the 21st Army Group with ground attack/close support cover. On 27 July 1944, 616 (South Yorkshire) Squadron AAF flew its first operational sortie with Meteor jet fighters (the first RAF unit to be so equipped) when it was sent to intercept and destroy German V1 rockets launched against southern England in general and London in particular.

RAF Waltham

Before the war, Waltham had been Grimsby's civil airfield, though it was used by the RAFVR and the air guard. It was in November 1941 that the first Wellington bombers moved in when 142 Squadron took up residence.

In February 1942, there was a change in units and aircraft with the arrival of 100 Squadron who were flying Lancaster MKIIIs.

Initially, Waltham had been a satellite for RAF Binbrook and known as RAF Grimsby (Waltham), but on 1 May 1943 the airfield was given official station status and was officially named RAF Grimsby four months later.

In October 1943 100 Squadron's C Flight was detached to the new airfield at Kelstern where it re-formed as 625 Squadron. A month later 100 Squadron spawned yet another new unit when C Flight was again detached, this time to form 550 Squadron who later moved to North Killingholm.

The airfield ceased operational duties on 2 April 1945 when the squadron and its aircraft moved to Elsham. Ten days later the base was put on a care and maintenance basis and later in the month Pioneer Corps units began moving in huge quantities of food to be dropped to starving Dutch civilians in what became known as Operation Manna.

153. Leading Aircraftman J A Skingsley with other members of a Wellington of 142 Squadron. Skingsley, who was acting flight engineer, was awarded the DFM for picking up a blazing oxygen bottle and throwing it out of the aircraft.

154. Waltham's most famous Lancaster *Able Mabel*, which went on to complete 121 operations with 100 Squadron. She was one of three bombers to top a hundred operations with the squadron. The squadron had its most disastrous night for losses on 16-17 December 1943, when 32 returning aircraft ran into bad weather. Firstly, *N-Nuts* crashed in flames at Kelstern followed by *H-Harry* at Barnolby. Then, as the others circled waiting for a break in the weather *Q-Queenie* and *F-Freddie* collided. There were just six survivors from four crews. The subsequent inquiry led to an arrangement with local searchlight units to guide bombers in bad weather.

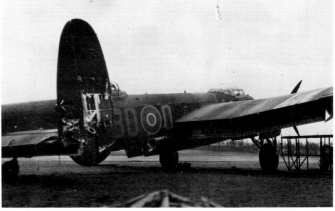

156-157. *Above:* 550 Squadron's *O-Oboe* sporting damage received from AA gunfire during a raid on Berlin. *Below:* 550 Squadron's *F-Fox* completed over one hundred operational missions. She is photographed here awaiting the starting signal to take-off.

159-160. 144 Squadron was adopted by Grimsby. *Above right:* A torpedo-carrying Beaufighter on an anti-shipping sortie. Beside its 'tin fish' the Beaufighter was armed with four cannon. *Below:* Ground crews preparing concrete torpedoes which Beaufighter pilots used on practise/training flights.

161-162. Loading a live torpedo on a Beaufighter of 144 Squadron. *Below:* On an operational sortie against enemy shipping.

163. Damaged turret in a bomber of 576 Squadron at RAF Elsham Wolds.

164. Swindon's adopted squadron was based at Elsham Wolds. Crews confer before setting off on a bombing mission over the Ruhr.

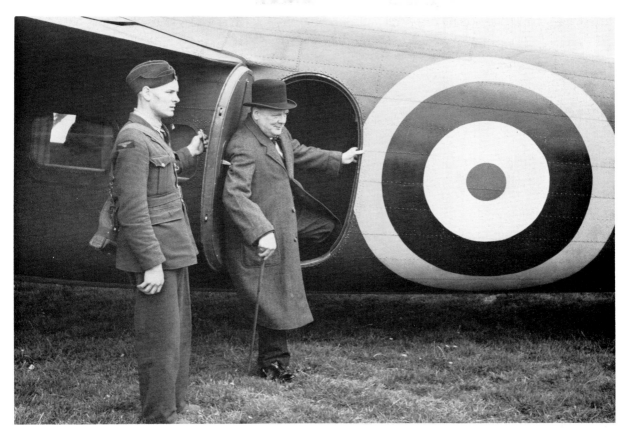

165-166. Winston Churchill pays a visit to RAF North Coates.

167-168. In May 1942 a Beaufighter Vlc ND-C left North Coates on a special mission. Her pilot, Flight Lieutenant Gatward, was charged with the task of flying at low-level to Paris where he was to drop a tricolour over the Arc de Triomphe. Fortunately for us, Flight Lieutenant Gatward took his camera along.

169. Flight Lieutenant Gatward's Beaufighter in which he made the daylight flight to Paris in May 1942.

171. 8 August 1944 and Beaufighters of 254 Squadron operating out of RAF North Coates launch an attack on a group of German minesweepers. The picture shows rocket projectiles streaking towards their target. The minesweepers were lying off Fromentine on the Biscay coast. Three out of the four ships attacked were hit and set on fire.

YOU
CAN HELP MAKE
ME A PLANE!
MOBILISE for
WAR WORK !

G727:
940.53
GR1

GRIMSBY
WINGS FOR VICTORY
TARGET : 'HALF-A-MILLION'
OFFICIAL PROGRAMME - Price 3d.

173. Grimsby's Wings for Victory Programme. Target £500,000.

174. Two Spitfires, *Grimsby I* and *II*, built with the £15,000 raised in the town. *Grimsby I* survived the war but the second machine paid for by Edwin Bacon — was lost over France in 1942.

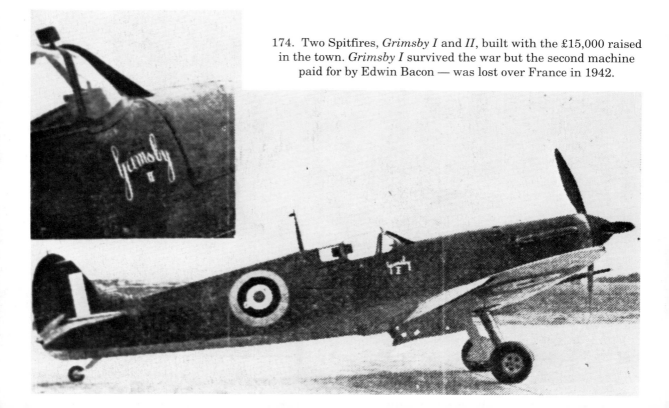

175. This captured Me109 was displayed in Town Hall Square, Grimsby, as part of the town's campaign to raise money to buy a Spitfire.

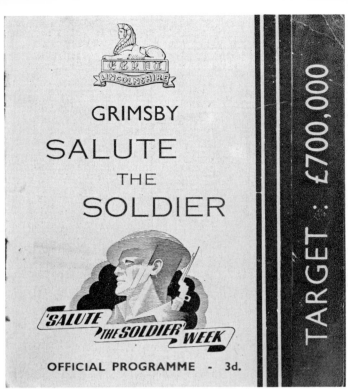

176. Salute The Soldier Week. Though the object of the exercise was to raise enough money to equip a battalion of the Lincolnshire Regiment, many of the concerts given during the campaign were performed by RAF bands.

177. 13 December 1943, and the stars and stripes fly over Grimsby to mark the first anniversary of the opening of the Red Cross Club (*see below*).

179-180. Men of Goxhill's Air Corps Supply looking exactly as everyone expects wartime GIs to look. *Below:* US airmen relaxing with their British girlfriends.

181. American servicemen relaxing in the sun at the junction of Pelham Road and Bargate in Grimsby.

182. Three American MPs and a serviceman, remembered as *Rosie* who hailed from New York, at the Red Cross Club.

183. Lighting up the sky for the Victory celebrations.

184. A Hitler effigy comes to a sticky end.

185. Residents of the Hope Street area, Grimsby, prepare the decorations after the announcement of VE Day.

187. Hanging out the washing on the Siegfried Line.

188. Granville Street and Heneage Road children's victory party held at Welholme Church Hall.

189. A family snapshot from the celebrations in Hope Street, Grimsby.

190. They went wild. Six long years of war went out of the window. In Grimsby and Cleethorpes it was party time.

191. Grimsby's deputy Mayor, Alderman Max Bloom, cuts the victory cake at a street party.

JAG SAUCE
...sh — it's good!

TOFFEE of the better kind
Wilkin's CREMONA

LIGHTING-UP TIME
9.40 p.m.   4.20 a.m.

Grimsby Evening Telegraph

LARGEST CERTIFIED NET SALES IN LINCOLNSHIRE

FINAL

No. 17,652   C   WEDNESDAY, AUGUST 8, 1945.   [REGISTERED AT THE GENERAL POST OFFICE AS A NEWSPAPER]   THREE-HALFPENCE

'All Living Things, Human and Animal, Seared To Death'

JAPS SAY HIROSHIMA IS A CITY OF RUINS

ATOMIC BOMB CLAIMED AS VIOLATION OF CONVENTION

'DEAD TOO NUMEROUS TO BE COUNTED'

HIROSHIMA is a city of ruins, and the dead are too numerous to be counted," Tokio radio said to-day, giving new details of the devastation caused by Atomic Bomb One.

Official Tokio quarters are now declaring that the use of the atomic bomb represents a violation of international law.

They recall that Article 22 of The Hague Convention makes it clear that attacks against towns are unforgivable actions.

"We ought to remember that they protested on numerous occasions in the name of humanity against the small-scale Japanese raids on London," adds the Jap radio.

"The destructive power of the bombs is indescribable," said the Japanese report. "It is impossible to distinguish between men and women who were near the fire.

"The destructive power of the bombs spread over a wide area."

An earlier Tokio broadcast picked up in New York to-day said that the atomic bomb "literally seared to death" all living things, human and animal, in Hiroshima.

The dead and injured were burned beyond recognition, and the authorities are unable to get any definite figure of civilian casualties.

The city was stated to be "a disastrous sight."

Tokio radio added: "The effect was wide-spread. Those outdoors were burned to death, while those indoors were killed by the indescribable pressure and heat.

"Houses and buildings smashed, including many medical facilities, the medical authorities have their hands full."

Pictures taken by American pilots after the raid show that 60 per cent. of Hiroshima was wiped out.

"OF CITY WIPED OUT WITH AWFUL THOROUGHNESS"

The atomic bomb dropped on Monday, which wiped out 60 per cent. of the area, was declared the Strategic Air Force in the Pacific.

NO COMPARISON

An American Strategic Air Force expert said there was no comparison between the atomic bomb fires and normal ones.

Yokohama looked as if whole sites were burning, whereas Hiroshima, a whole plume rose many thousands of feet into the air.

The lower part of the city, with the dock and harbour facilities, appeared to be barely touched by the tremendous concussion, the expert said.

The U.S. Navy Department has given the Japanese a radio warning that they must now take their chance of mass suicide or surrender. We may have to devastate four or five cities before...

U.S. THINKING OF ATOMIC ROCKETS

The American military authorities are already studying the possibilities of the U.S. being attacked by atomic rockets, either from Europe or from Asia, said New York radio to-day.

A competent military observer was quoted as saying that "Hiroshima was selected rather than Tokio so as to save as many lives as possible, while giving ample demonstration of the missile's power."—Reuter.

Corp. Thomas Reynolds, of South Shields, and Miss Irene Smith, of Lawson-avenue, Grimsby, married at Grimsby Registry Office.

ATOMIC BOMB—A SCIENTIST'S WARNING

A WARNING of the disaster which mankind might bring against measureless catastrophe, was given to-day by Sir Henry Hallett Dale, President of the Royal Society and chairman of the Scientific Advisory Committee to the War Cabinet since 1942.

FINAL DISASTER

INVASION PLANS UNCHANGED

GUAM, Wednesday.
The perfection of the atomic bomb has had no changed Allied plans for the invasion of Japan, it is understood here.

Preparations for amphibious landings continue.

Troops are still being deployed from the Euro-pean theatre to Pacific bases, where supplies and material are being rushed to the places where they are most needed.—Reuter.

END OF SECRECY

"NEW AND BRUTAL WEAPON"

AT LONG RANGE

RUSSIANS STIRRED

MOSCOW, Wednesday.

GARDEN FETE AT LOUTH

Fancy Dress Parade Prizewinners

The Bank Holiday garden fete held in the Priory Grounds, Louth, in aid of the Borough of Louth Sailors, Soldiers and Airmen's Welfare Fund, was fortunately marred by the weather, but it provided enjoyment to quite a number of people.

Coun. F. W. Macdonald presided at the opening ceremony, which was performed by the Mayor (Coun. J. R. Sanderson).

JAPAN'S MAIN STEEL CITY STRUCK TO-DAY

GENERAL SPAATZ'S Super Fortresses, filling in Japan's "days of grace" between atomic bomb No. 1 and the expected second strike, continued attacks to-day, and rained high explosives on Yawata, on Japan's biggest steel city, and one of the last group of towns to be warned in Saturday's leaflet raid.

GENERALLY EXCELLENT

A MODEST START

MOUNTAIN PUSH IN NEW GUINEA

MELBOURNE, Wednesday.
After two days of artillery concentration, Australian troops in New Guinea have fought farther up the southern slopes of the Prince Alexander mountains.

RAIL WAGE CLAIM

Decisive Stage To-day ?

The rail talks which began over a week ago are expected to reach a decisive stage to-day.

WOMEN'S BOWLS CHAMPION

Grimsby West End Club's Annual Fixture

FOR THE HOME

PARTING GIFTS TO MINISTER

Grimsby Central Hall Presentations

FRENCH CHILDREN'S HOLIDAY IN GERMANY

BOWRING

REMINDER !

There is no finer COD LIVER OIL in the world than that produced in your own port.

COMPARE THE STANDARD with any other advertised oils : VITAMIN A 25,000 I.U.   VITAMIN D 2,500 I.U. per ounce. Yet this Fine Grimsby Oil produced by Bowring's costs you no more.

The Sole Area Distributors are FAIRBANK KIRBY, Ltd.

ASK YOUR CHEMIST FOR

GRIMSBY

SILVER MEDAL BRAND

PURE FRESH COD LIVER OIL

OUR CONFIDENCE IN GRIMSBY'S FUTURE

GOLDEN WEDDING RECORDS

Unusual Reunion at Grimsby

"SECRET AGREEMENT" EVIDENCE IN PARIS TO-DAY

From HAROLD KING, Reuter's Special Correspondent

PARIS, Wednesday.
GENERAL BERGERET, Vichy Minister of Air, and Admiral Blehaut, Vichy Navy Minister, who left France with Marshal Petain when he went to Germany last April are expected to be brought from Fresnes prison to-day to give evidence at Petain's trial entering on its 13th day.

11,200 JAP LOSSES IN BURMA

S.E.A.C. H.Q., KANDY, Ceylon, Wednesday.

SCARTHOE WOMEN'S GUILD

Entertainment and Instruction

BRITISH AND RUSSIAN FORCES TO LEAVE TEHERAN

TEHERAN, Wednesday.
THE Foreign Ministry announced to-day that the British Embassy has informed it that "it was decided at Potsdam that the British and Russian forces are to be withdrawn from Teheran at once.

Leopold Herman, Reuter's correspondent in Teheran, cables:—
The news was received with great satisfaction by all Persian circles who are that the Allies are evacuating their troops from the capital before they are actually obliged to do so under the Tripartite Treaty.

EUROPE'S 'GRIM WINTER'

U.N.R.R.A.'s Pressing Need

GRAIN EXPLOSION SHAKES TWO CITIES

PORT ARTHUR (Ontario), Wednesday.
Two cities ten miles (Port Arthur and Fort William) were rocked by the explosion which wrecked 2,000,000-bushel wheat elevator on the waterfront yesterday.

WEATHER MIXTURE AS BEFORE

Weather forecast for 24 hours commencing noon :—
General Inference : A shallow depression centred over the North Midlands is moving slowly south over England.

Continued from Previous Column

COUPONS—146 PLUS—HELP ATS INTO CIVVY STREET

A-PLANES — "DISTINCT POSSIBILITY"

WASHINGTON, Wednesday.

193. V J Night. At last it is *all* over.

194. The spoils of war. A surrendered U-boat on public display at Grimsby Royal Dock.

195-196. Thanksgiving Week parade. *Below:* The Mayor gets to grips with a 20mm AA gun mounted on an Admiralty trawler.

197-198. Remembrance Day, 11 November 1945

199-200. Remembrance Day, 11 November 1945

201. Planning the war memorial at Cleethorpes, 19 February 1946.

202. Demolishing a surface air raid shelter in Grimsby. 27 April 1946.

203. Going . . . going . . . gone. Sale of surplus civil defence equipment at Augusta Street Barracks.

204. Bridge-laying tank passes the old Prince of Wales Hotel, Grimsby. Victory Parade.

205. Part of the Victory Parade pictured in Freeman Street, Grimsby. The fuselage section of a Dakota passes Marks & Spencers.)

CHEERS !

Top: Victory party at Imperial Avenue
Centre: The 1st Cleethorpes Girls Training Corps, 1941
Bottom: HMS *Scorpion* rounding the Humber Lightship